Trailer Park Parable

A Memoir of How
Three Brothers
Strove to Rise
Above Their
Broken Past,
Find Forgiveness,
and Forge a
Hopeful Future

Tyler Zed

Post Hill
PRESS

A POST HILL PRESS BOOK
ISBN: 979-8-88845-192-2
ISBN (eBook): 979-8-88845-193-9

Trailer Park Parable:
A Memoir of How Three Brothers Strove to Rise Above Their Broken
Past, Find Forgiveness, and Forge a Hopeful Future
© 2024 by Tyler Zed
All Rights Reserved

Cover design by Cody Corcoran

All people, locations, events, and situations are portrayed to the best of the author's memory. While all of the events described are true, some names and identifying details have been changed to protect the privacy of the people involved.

Post Hill Press
New York • Nashville
posthillpress.com

Published in the United States of America
1 2 3 4 5 6 7 8 9 10

For Grandpa Ervin Olson

AUTHOR'S NOTE

Many of you are reading this because you heard about the book from my YouTube channel, Zeducation. Over the five years the channel has existed, more than 1 million people have subscribed, and the videos have amassed 300 million total views. It has been nothing but a dream making content and having people watch and enjoy it, and I am forever grateful for the support of the viewers. It's almost the exact dream my buddies and I envisioned when we were kids. But my hope is that this story reaches many who have never heard of Zeducation and may not even be interested in that type of content.

Although this story is not about the channel, it is about an event and its aftermath that shaped my family's future and what you see on the channel today. It's about mental health, addiction, and tragedy. It's about perseverance, faith, and most importantly about prioritizing and always being there for the people in your life.

To write this book, I relied on my own memories and recollection of events.

The following names are pseudonyms: Akwonde, Coach Hock, Dream, Emma, Huey, James, Master Sergeant Denson, Sergeant Laquon White, and Sergeant Johnson. Jerry Zimmer is a composite character.

Another pseudonym is my own. Many of you know me as Tyler Zed, but my real name is Desmond Janousek.

CHAPTER 1

DECEMBER 28TH, 2007

Four days had passed since I thought I'd witnessed my mom die. For those entire four days I sat and listened to music by myself, wondering if Mom was going to be okay and still in shock at what had happened on Christmas Eve. Replaying it all in my head, frame by frame. Over and over and over.

I was seventeen, my brother Devin was sixteen, and Beau was eleven. We sat outside Mom's hospital room waiting to go in and see her. My heart raced. I didn't know what to expect or what to say to her. I don't remember exactly who spoke, but someone told the three of us to "be prepared to see your mom in rough shape, it's not good." And they weren't kidding. As we walked in I saw Mom sitting up in the hospital bed. I only knew it was her because I heard her say, "Hi guys," and it was her voice, but her face was unrecognizable. It was black and blue, one of her eyes was completely swollen shut, and the other had blood in it. Never in my life had I felt so many emotions at once. Anger, guilt, worry, and relief to see my mom and see her alive.

I sat on one side of the bed, and my brothers sat on the other side. Whoever let us in had closed the door behind us, and for the first time in four days it was just the four of us again, alone. I could feel the lump in my throat growing and the tears welling up. I did everything I could to hold them in. I needed to be strong.

Don't cry, don't cry, don't cry I kept telling myself.

MARCH 2011

When we are kids we think that the adults around us know everything. It took me until I was twenty to fully understand that there is no such thing as a grown-up.

I was just starting basic training in Texas, and all around me grown men were crying. I held a little piece of paper in front of my face, waiting to read it off word for word as the phone rang in my ear. It was the first week, and one of the silly things the trainers do to stress out new recruits is give them a piece of paper with a script to read. Then the MTIs (military training instructors) tell them to call home for the first time, but the new recruits can only read from the script. No other words at all. If they say anything else, the MTIs yell at you while you're on the phone with your loved ones and make you hang up on them. The paper was only about three sentences long, and it said something like, "I made it safely, this is my address." It was a very simple text to read, but more than half of the guys in my flight of sixty couldn't handle it.

I looked around and tears were flowing as they tried to read the script. Grown men in their twenties crying like children talking to their moms and wives, wanting to say more but not being able to while the MTIs sat ready to pounce. One kid started straying from his script, and I heard, "What the frick! That's not what that says. Read the damn paper!" The kid cried harder, and another MTI sprinted from across the room and started yelling at him too. The MTIs loved that. At the first sign of a trainee pissing themselves in fear or discomfort, the MTIs all turned into vultures and jumped on the fresh meat.

"Grown-ass men crying! You miss mommy?! Unbelievable. This goddamn generation. Pussies. We are so screwed against China whenever that happens." One of the MTIs shook his head as he walked by me.

"Hello?" I heard Mom's voice. I quickly snapped my eyes back from across the room to my piece of paper, but first I made sure there were no MTIs around me before I spoke.

"Mom?" I said. "I'm supposed to read this card, but just grab a pen really quick. I have an address for you. Miss and love you guys, can't say anything else—" An MTI turned around. I started reading the script before he heard me say more. "My mailing address is the following..."

Never once did a tear well up. Call me a non-pussified millennial, but it seemed like a pretty silly thing to cry over. I knew Mom would understand, and it's not that I didn't miss her or home, but I knew all of this was temporary, and so did she. I would get to call home again at some point and be able to explain, and if she had questions there are a million forums online that talk about this exact phone call.

After hanging up, I stood at attention and waited until everyone was done with their calls, watching others get yelled at and others cry. This was not what I had expected at all when I'd left for basic training, but this seemed to be the theme of that first week, finding out that I'd had a warped idea of what my experience would be like.

I was expecting to be surrounded by dozens of guys running six-minute miles, doing a hundred push-ups with ease, and walking around emotionless like military robots. I had been worried that I didn't do enough to prepare myself. This was not the case. I was well prepared to handle basic, if not overprepared. I don't say that braggingly either. My perception of basic training and the military were far from reality. I had clearly watched too many Navy SEAL movies, and I think this happens with many people who join with certain high expectations. I also didn't realize at the time that my upbringing had overprepared me for this kind of emotional manipulation. It's part of the reason my peers called me "the perfect trainee," graduating with honors and excelling at almost everything we did. Our upbringing also helped my brother Beau graduate number one in his Navy basic training class. Literally number one out of 1,200 recruits in his unit. To say that I was proud as hell of him is an understatement. We didn't know why at the time, but we were perfect candidates to handle the emotional game of the military—more than prepared—and I'm not sure if that's a good thing or a bad thing.

I want to clarify that basic training wasn't "easy." I hear a lot of people say, "Oh yea, it was a cakewalk, basic is a joke," but the truth is it's subjective, and it's not a "cakewalk," no matter who you are. It's definitely a lot easier than I thought it would be, but it still isn't two months I would voluntarily go back and relive. It was a mental game, and the entire point of basic training in any branch is to detach you from your previous life and identity and make you prioritize your new identity: that of a soldier, marine, airman, or sailor. These new military duties will deal with life and death situations, and attention to detail is a must. Worrying about your individual lifestyle, ethnicity, religion, and so on, gets in the way of that. There is no time for that in the military—you either grow the hell up and get over all of that or get out. There's a mission, and the mission comes first. For some people, that is hard to do depending on what their previous life was like.

That being said, there is a clear difference between Marine basic training and the rest, and for good reason. Marines are out there getting shot at and shooting far more than the other branches. To get someone mentally prepared for that experience is tough, so the mental training is tougher. My friend was a Marine, and he said that during the first week at boot camp, the Drill Instructors told the new recruits that North Korea had attacked America and that they would all be deploying in the following few weeks, even though they'd just arrived and hadn't even shot a weapon yet. The new recruits had no idea how to confirm this, either, because in basic you are completely cut off from the outside world. "America needed the bodies" they were told, and they were all going to war the next day. Talk about a mind screw. The mental games in Air Force basic training were nowhere near that level, but they still existed.

The entire driving force of the military is fear. You do what you are supposed to because you fear the repercussions of not doing what you are supposed to. One way they try to teach you this principle is by public humiliation. There is no greater driving force in our lives than peer pressure and trying to fit in with the people around you, at least for a large majority of the population. Looking foolish in front of your peers is humiliating, but letting your peers down and seeing them suffer because of you is even more humiliating. Getting yelled at in basic isn't fun, but if you are the weak link out in the operational military, the punishment for failure is far worse than embarrassment. Don't let your team down. Do your damn job and do it right all the way down to the tiny details. The consequences could be life and death.

Some people are able to fall in line with this concept, and others are just meant to be weak links.

That brings me to Akwonde and Huey. Both came in with soft lives before the military, but one could adapt and one couldn't.

Akwonde was around thirty years old and from Nigeria. This guy couldn't march or do push-ups to save his life, and every time he messed up, the rest of the flight got smoked for it. We would either have to do push-ups or flutter kicks while Akwonde stood at attention and watched us, and he felt bad for failing us (at least that was the goal of the instructors). The psychology behind it is to get the rest of us pissed at Akwonde for not performing and for Akwonde to succumb to the peer pressure and the fear of letting everyone down again so he would do everything right the next time.

I hated Akwonde for the first few weeks. We got smoked all the time because of him, doing extra push-ups and flutter kicks. I wanted so badly for him to just quit so we didn't have to suffer because of him ever again.

Around the fourth week, I was put on door watch with Akwonde. Two people had to be on door watch at all times in each flight. During the day, they let people in and out of the dorm as they came and went, and at night, they made their rounds to make sure everyone was in their beds. The Air Force made two people do it instead of one so that a person who may have been feeling a little blue didn't off themselves. Dark, but it's the truth.

Two guys at all times, and I was finally paired with Akwonde at around 2 a.m.

As much as I disliked the guy, I wasn't going to be a dick and not talk to him during our two hours together.

"So what's your story, man? What did you do before this?" I asked him.

"I ran my own business in New York City," he said in his very thick African accent. He and his wife had moved from Nigeria to New York, where he'd owned five hotdog stands. But in his tribe in Nigeria, his family was some sort of royalty. He was driven around with chauffeurs, and his family had butlers his entire life, which explained why he was softer than baby poo at doing anything physical. Surprisingly, I never saw the guy cry, for which I gave him credit.

"So why did you leave that life?" I asked. "Sounds like you pretty much had it made."

I then learned that his wife was a member of a different tribe and apparently that was a big no-no, especially with the status of his family. His family gave him an ultimatum: it was either her or the family. If he chose her, he had to leave.

He picked her, and they moved to America to live their lives together. A few years later, Akwonde joined the Air Force to get his citizenship.

"I love this country, man. It has given me so much," he told me that night.

From that day forward I never felt an ounce of animosity toward Akwonde. I had a lot of respect for him after hearing his story, and, after I saw that he was improving by leaps and bounds in the physical part of training, I respected him even more. Whenever we had a task, I would ask him if he needed my help, and he started doing the same for me. At the end, Akwonde still wasn't ripping out one hundred push-ups in a minute, and he wasn't the perfect marcher, but he definitely was not the worst and was probably the most improved. He was also my friend and my fellow American, after they granted his citizenship for his service to this country, which was well earned.

Some people shouldn't be in the military, period. Although Akwonde wasn't necessarily military ready at the start, he *wanted* to be there and he wanted to get better and he wanted to be a part of the team. That is enough to take someone on and give them a chance, and he over delivered at the end.

That brings me to Baby Huey. He was someone who shouldn't have made it past the doormat at the recruiter's office in New York, but sadly represents about 20 to 30 percent of the military population today (in my experience).

Huey's real name isn't important because from day one the MTIs saw this twenty-year-old's baby face, and all they called him was Baby Huey. I haven't pinned it down, but it was either the baby face that painted the target on him or the tracksuit and bushy mullet he arrived in, or the chocolate candy bar crusted on his lips (not kidding), or the two giant suitcases filled with household items like an iron and a gallon of laundry detergent, or maybe it was his bag-of-milk body that looked like it hadn't left the gaming chair until he left to join the Air Force. Roughly 29 percent of the US population aged eighteen to twenty-four is eligible to join the military. This kid was not a part of that 29 percent and was visibly a recruiter's desperate attempt to meet his quota. Unlike Akwonde, there was also no will within Huey to get better and adapt.

Before I tell how Baby Huey fared, I need to tell you about our MTI.

I had a lot of respect for Sergeant White. He was from South Carolina and proud as hell to be in the Air Force. He didn't want to see it getting soft (like the military absolutely is today in 2024, something that should concern every American).

I don't know if this was a planned mind game or not, but all of us got off the airplane in San Antonio, onto the bus, and were driven onto the base to our dormitory. When we arrived, I thought for about six hours that it was going to be a cakewalk.

When we stopped at our dorm, a different MTI got on the bus and calmly said, "Everyone off the bus with your bags and go stand on a yellow dot." We all scurried off the bus and over to a yellow dot on the pavement. From there, the MTI calmly told us to "lift your bag, set your bag down, and say 'Proceeding sir' as you do it." That game lasted about ten minutes. Finally, he had us go up into the dorm and into what they called a "day room." It was just a big, open tiled room with chairs pushed up against the walls (which you were not allowed to sit in). We had to sit cross-legged on the floor facing a whiteboard at the front.

That night, there was something that baffled me. Something didn't feel right. I tried, but failed, to connect some dots. The soft-spoken MTI was a pretty small guy, probably about 5'9" and 160 pounds. He didn't yell once. For a few hours he had us filling out paperwork and telling us rules. I honestly thought that if this guy was going to be leading me for eight weeks it would be a mini vacation. But the thing that wasn't clicking was that draped over the chairs that lined the walls in the day room were t-shirts that said, "325 pound bench press club… 375 pound bench press club… 450 pound bench press club… 500 pound bench press club." These t-shirts couldn't belong to this guy. If this guy could get up 225, I'd be shocked. As I laid down to sleep, I concluded that basic training with a guy so soft spoken couldn't be legit.

It wasn't.

At 4 a.m., I awoke to, "Wake the hell up! Line up in the hallway right now! Hurry up!" As I jumped out of bed and put on my shoes, I saw who the "500 pound bench press club" t-shirt belonged to. It belonged to The Hulk from South Carolina, Sergeant Laquon White. His brow bent as he screamed, telling us to get in the hallway "quick, fast, and in a hurry!" We weren't moving fast enough, and he flipped a few mattresses. I was ready for him to punch right through the cinderblock walls if we didn't somehow move faster.

This was the basic training I had expected, at least the hard-nosed badass yelling at me. This guy was what the military should strive to be, a hard-nosed badass, and I still think that to this day.

That first day was a lot of yelling and trying to pick out the weaklings in the flight so attention could be directed where it needed to be, which brings me to the moment Sergeant White identified Baby Huey as the top weakling.

During that first day, we were outside doing push-ups, flutter kicks, and up downs. After most of us were gassed, Sergeant White took on a calm tone. "All right, I know there are some of you who thought this was a mistake and you are rethinking your decision to join the military. I will give all of you this one chance to back out and head home, no repercussions. No penalty. If you don't think this is for you, then now is the time to say so. Just stand up and line up over on the pavement and we will start the paperwork. You can go back home tonight."

He seemed very sincere, and to five guys in our flight, he sounded sincere enough to go line up on the pavement. Huey was one of those five.

The five stood there at attention. Sergeant White paced in front of them. "All right, you five don't think you have it, huh? I see." He looked back at the rest of us with a smirk. "Well, there ain't no quitting! The rest of you get to do push-ups because of the dream team here!"

We got smoked more because of the five who wanted to quit. Not only were those five targeted by the MTIs the rest of the time, they were also off on the wrong foot with the rest of the flight.

All five shouldn't have been in the military to begin with. Hell, they were emotionally weak enough to want to quit on the first day. The MTIs were either going to mold them into doing their jobs, or they were going to get these guys out of the military one way or the other, and all of this involved making their lives hell.

Week after week, Huey struggled to get right. He couldn't. He sucked at everything. I should also say that one of the other ways they make trainees fearful is by threatening them that they will be "washed back" in training. If the MTIs think you are struggling and think you need more time in basic, they will wash you back to a flight that may be a week or even several weeks earlier in training, meaning you'd have to repeat all the lessons and stay in basic training longer than expected.

In basic training, getting washed back is the ultimate humiliation.

I feel no sympathy for Huey and his lack of will and ability, but the way he went was questionable, and it was the only time I didn't do what my MTI told me to; to this day part of me agrees with what Sergeant White did, and part of me doesn't.

Every single person who had contact with him knew that Huey didn't belong.

It was the sixth week, only two weeks left. We were all getting ready to graduate and head to our tech schools to start training for our jobs. As we were in the middle of our daily tasks, we heard Sergeant White yell, "All right, everyone line up in the hallway, right now!" We did as we were told. At the end of the hallway, I saw Huey packing up his locker into his green duffel bag. Tears were rolling down his cheeks.

"Airman Huey is finally getting washed back," Sergeant White said. Huey turned with his duffel bag and started walking toward us, all of us lined up making a tunnel to the door. Tears increased as Huey held his chin down to his chest.

"All right everyone, as Huey leaves us and gets washed back to week three, give him a farewell."

The flight broke out singing the chorus of Steam's "Na Na Hey Hey Kiss Him Goodbye."

I didn't.

I stood at attention and watched Huey cry his eyes out as he exited the dorm, headed to his new flight.

Looking back, I think Sergeant White was giving him one final humiliation before his new flight. Huey would either figure it all out and start contributing to the team, or he got to feel that terrible humiliation again.

The other part of me knew that Huey didn't have a chance, and he should have been kicked out of the military right then and there. Stomping him into the ground with more humiliation didn't make sense to me. This was further than it needed to be.

None of this changed my mind about Sergeant White. When it comes to a life and death situation, there's almost nobody I'd trust more. In fact, it only made me question my own sanity: why did I not participate in singing? Why did I empathize with this sack of lard named Huey? Did Huey deserve any sympathy at all?

DECEMBER 28TH, 2007

Sitting on Mom's hospital bed, I looked up at her. To that point, I had managed to hold back the tears and swallow the lump in my throat. After seeing what he'd done to her face I had to look away again. The lump in my throat came back, and the tears welled once more. I didn't want to cry and be weak when Mom needed us most. When my brothers needed me to be strong now. I looked at both of my brothers, and I knew they were thinking the same thing as me. I could see the lumps in their throats as they fought to hold back the tears too.

I couldn't look back at Mom or I'd let it all out.

For a few moments, we sat there. Together in our new broken reality.

"It's okay to cry," Mom said.

In an instant, all three of us embraced our mom, and the four of us cried. I held onto my brothers and my mom as tight as I could.

CHAPTER 2

WHEN YOU'RE A KID, WHATEVER REALITY IS SERVED UP IN FRONT of your face is "normal." You have nothing else to compare your life to. Unwilfully ignorant and unaware of what else is there. "Normal" is whatever you are given.

The normal for Jerry Zimmer was that of being a stinky, poorly dressed outcast since the day he'd moved to my town and joined my fifth-grade class. When I tell you he stunk, I mean it. He smelled like some strain of dried piss on most days, and, as a fifth grade kid, that was predictably bad for his social standing. On the playground, the girls would play "Jerry Cooties" and run away from whoever was designated the one with Jerry's cooties. Jerry would get in on the kickball games with us boys, but if it weren't for his ability to kick a decent ball, then we probably wouldn't have let him play.

Outside of kickball, Jerry didn't have much social interaction with our class, and it got even worse for him. It was a Monday, and from the moment we all got to school we smelled it. It was a rancid stench of rotten eggs and moldy vomit fumigating the whole place. Before class started, the principal located the source of the sour smell: full milk cartons had been sitting over the weekend in Jerry's locker. I don't know what he did at recess that week, but after the stink bomb he surely wasn't playing kickball with us, probably out of fear of getting razzed again.

It was about two weeks after the milk carton incident that Jerry sent out his birthday invitations. He gave everyone in class an invitation, about twenty kids. I put it in my backpack and didn't think twice about going. I didn't want to go to Jerry's birthday party and then be called a stinker too. Mom found the invitation and set it aside while we did homework.

Two weeks went by, and on a Saturday I came upstairs in the morning to find a present sitting on the kitchen table. When I asked whose it was, she said, "Your friend Jerry's. Remember his party is in about an hour?"

"Mom, Jerry is not my friend," I said. "I'm not going to his party. He stinks!"

Mom looked at me with scorn, and when she scorns you, you know she's not messing around. The hairs on my neck quickly stood up. I never messed with Mom and that look. "How would you feel if you invited him to your party and he didn't show up? You need to treat others how you want to be treated. I don't care if you think he stinks. You're going."

Off I reluctantly went to Jerry's party, and we were late, which made things worse on the way there. First I was going to be a jerk and not go, then I dragged my feet... Mom was not happy with my attitude. *At least my friends will be there*, I thought.

When I walked into the Wendy's restaurant, none of my friends were there. In fact, nobody was. Just Jerry sitting by himself at the table of placemats with his four-year-old sister running around.

Nobody else besides me would show up.

I remember a few other things from that day. I remember eating Wendy's, then going to watch *Shrek* at the theater, then playing with Legos at Jerry's house until I got picked up. Plus, Jerry's house had that same awful smell we always smelled at school. His mom made us a snack, and when she opened the fridge I saw milk cartons from school, the same kind that Jerry had let musk in his locker over the weekend. I also remember that I had a fun time. I didn't even think about the smell after a while.

When I left, Dad told me that Jerry's family heated their house with wood and that sometimes burning certain wood gives off a bad smell, especially if the house isn't properly ventilated. That explained Jerry's stink. I couldn't figure out the milk carton thing at the time, but later realized Jerry's family was poor as dirt and he was stealing cartons at lunch and milk break to bring home to his family. Unfortunately for him, he just forgot to bring them home one Friday.

For the rest of the time throughout grade school, I was never close with Jerry, but I never left him out of kickball and told others to stop teasing him about his smell. Jerry's piss smell came from the wood heater, I told them, like I was some sort of expert on wood furnaces.

Jerry's "normal" was getting made fun of for stinking like piss, because of something he had no control of, and nobody showing up at his party. Humiliation. Normal was his poor wood-heated trailer house and gambling-addicted, chain-smoking parents who helped them stay poor. He didn't know any different. None of us do growing up.

Like Jerry, I thought everything I grew up with was how almost everyone was raised. I thought everyone was scared to death of their dads and that their moms cried about their scary dads and that every adult loved that nasty beer taste with their pills. I didn't start realizing until I was fourteen that the "normal" at my house wasn't what everyone else had.

Growing up, my parents told us that we had to do something for each season of the year. "You're not sitting at home playing video games," they would say. We either had to play a sport, play an instrument, or do a club at school. That started very early, and I am thankful every day that this was one of their rules. I played football in the fall, baseball in the spring and summer, and I rotated between guitar lessons, wrestling, and basketball in the winter. Devin also played football and baseball and in the winters did wrestling, basketball, and played piano and violin. Beau was quite a bit younger than us, so he didn't get the same treatment in these seasonal activity rules.

Devin and I both did well at our sports, and a lot of that had to do with our dad pushing us to be good. I definitely give that to him. Dads should be hard on their sons to a degree, but sometimes when we got yelled at for playing poorly, it just didn't feel right. I didn't see other kids' parents doing and saying what he did.

Our dad would take us to the baseball field to practice pitching, which was amazing that I had a dad who would do that for us—many kids don't—but we'd leave after about three pitches because we couldn't throw a strike. "Throw a fuckin' strike or we're leaving," he'd say. The pressure would be on, and then I'd throw one in the dirt, it would hit my dad's shin, the F-bombs would drop, and we'd be headed home. The rest of the evening would be all of us walking on eggshells at the possibility that he would still be pissed and lash out, all for not throwing a strike during the three-pitch practice at the age of ten.

This had different effects on my brother and me. My dad acting like that made me want to do well so I didn't have to see him pissed off, and I was usually one of the best players on all of my teams because of that, all the way through high school. It was also equally rewarding when I was the best player because my dad was proud as hell. One of the first times I realized that I could get that reaction from him was in fifth grade, when I intercepted a pass and ran it back for a touchdown at the end of the game. My dad grabbed me on the sideline and raised me into the air as high as he could as everyone on my team cheered. It was a great feeling throughout the rest of the weekend. My dad was happy at home and we didn't have to walk on eggshells, my friends liked me for it, the girls in my class fawned over it. I wanted to keep feeling that good feeling, so I kept getting better and better so that I could.

I know Devin wanted to do well, too, but when we were nine and ten years old, instead of channeling the humiliation our dad made us feel, Devin would cry on the pitcher's mound when Dad yelled at him. When he would start crying, Dad would start yelling more in front of the entire crowd and other players. It just snowballed the humiliating feeling and caused Devin to withdraw and rebel against what Dad wanted him to do. Devin didn't want to play anymore. He didn't want to feel that anymore, and I don't blame him.

The years Dad would coach us, the other parents didn't even want their kids playing for him. One day we were at the baseball park, and Mom was talking to another mom who said she would "never let her son play for that one coach. The way he talks to and treats his players is not okay." That "one coach" was my dad.

I still wonder why and how Dad ever got like that. Why did he treat us like that? Did he have good intentions for us? Was it stemming from his own insecurities? What was his dad like with him? His grandfather to his dad?

The best assumption I have is that most of the emotional abuse and bipolar mood swings stemmed from substance addiction.

Mom did her best to shield us from stuff, but eventually it all became too much. One day, I walked into the laundry room and found her bawling her eyes out, pacing, and mumbling, "I can't, I just can't anymore. I can't take it." I knew what she couldn't take, but I didn't know all of it. Mom hid a lot from us for our own good. She wanted to give us a normal family life, so she battled through the BS, trying to give that to us.

For the longest time, I thought Dad just liked to drink beer. When I was twelve, on our traveling baseball trips, he would drink with two of the other dads until 1 or 2 a.m. to the point where he was stumbling and incoherent. Then we'd have a game at 8 a.m., and he'd still be half in the bag. When Dad drank, he got goofy, not like the other dads. It was uncomfortable for everyone.

When I was fourteen, I realized he was definitely using something else besides just alcohol.

It was around 10 a.m. in the summertime. Dad was still asleep. Our phone rang, and I answered.

"Hi, this is the orthodontist. Are you coming in? You were supposed to be here a half hour ago, but if you can still make it, all we need is you and a parent to sign the paperwork so we can put on your braces next week."

Dang, I thought. Late for the appointment, Mom was at work, and now I had to go wake up Dad to take me. *He's going to be mad as hell*, I thought, but I had no choice. If I didn't wake him up and delayed the appointment then he'd be mad at me for that. It was a lose-lose situation.

"Dad," I said as I opened his bedroom door.

He was sitting on the side of the bed, swaying, his eyes closed.

"Dad?" I said concerned.

He snapped his head. "Yea. Just a second!"

When we left, I didn't notice anything really wrong. All I thought about was what his mood would be later in the day, after this inconvenience to his morning. The orthodontist's office was about ten minutes away, and, at the first stoplight, I realized something wasn't right with him.

When the light turned green, I stayed looking forward, waiting for him to start driving, but he didn't.

The car behind us honked, and the light turned red again before he could go.

I looked over at him, and he was asleep. His eyelids were fluttering. Mouth wide open like someone drooling in ecstasy.

The car behind us honked again as we sat at the red light.

Dad snapped up to look in the rearview mirror, eyes heavy.

"Ffffuuugh you honk for? Go to hell," he said.

"Dad, you missed the green light," I said, immediately regretting saying it.

"I di-n't miss the light!" he slurred. I stared straight forward, knowing if I said anything else I'd get yelled at again.

He somehow managed to get us to the orthodontist's office in one piece, falling asleep a few more times at the lights but not missing any green ones.

When we entered the waiting room, I saw one of the girls from my class and three other kids and their parents.

"Hi. We're late, sorry about that," I said to the receptionist.

"Not a problem!" she said. "Just take a seat, and we will be right with you."

I turned around to take a seat and saw my dad already sitting... Well, slouched on the chair, drooling, eyes fluttering again. He was clearly messed up, and everyone in the waiting room could tell. I made eye contact with the pretty girl from my class and quickly shifted my eyes to the ground. I felt humiliated. *Please fricking call us back soon,* I thought. I wanted to crawl into a damn hole.

We sat for about five minutes before getting called back, but it felt like an hour. I got up to follow the receptionist and was so eager to leave the waiting room that I forgot to make sure Dad was with me. I looked back and he was still sitting there with his eyes closed.

"Dad," I said in front of the room.

He snapped up. "Yeah. I'm coming," he said, irritated, thankfully restraining the curses this time.

As soon as he sat down, an assistant showed us a few slides talking about my braces, the insurance, and the follow-up appointments. For a few slides, I had hope that he would make it through without falling asleep again. But he didn't. The receptionist noticed, and I tapped his leg before she said anything. She shot me a look of concern, then rushed through the rest of the slides and set a piece of paper in front of Dad to sign.

"All right, sir, just sign this and you guys are good to go for the braces next week. I will be right back."

She left the room for a second, and when she returned, Dad was sitting with the pen in his hand, the paper still unsigned, and his head drooping, almost hitting the table as his drool-face and fluttering eyes came back.

"Sir!" she said and looked at me again.

Dad snapped up, signed the paper, and when I say signed the paper, he might have managed two lines. Nothing close to his real signature or even an English letter.

We got up and walked out, and as I did, I caught one last look from the assistant as if she was saying, "I'm sorry."

I caught my classmate's eyes on the way out, and again, I snapped them to the floor and put my chin to my chest. The last thing I wanted to do after this embarrassing show was face my classmates when school started back up.

On the drive home, he fell asleep at a few more lights and I got yelled at a few more times for waking him up. We got home, and he went into his room and closed the door.

I didn't tell my mom that story when she got home—it would have just been one more thing for her to worry about—but when I told my brother Devin, he said, "Dude, he did the same thing when I rode with him the other day. He was hitting himself in the head and plucking at his hairs trying to stay awake."

That was when I finally and undoubtedly realized that this wasn't everyone else's "normal." This was messed up.

I didn't see anyone act like Dad did that day until years later when I had a patient in the military who was addicted to opiates.

Like Jerry, our "normal" was not the popular norm. Unlike Jerry, for most of my childhood, my home norm was not visible to the outside world. Jerry had to walk around with his stink and poor clothes. Unless you saw my dad when he was messed up, you probably didn't know anything was off at my house. Luckily for my brothers and me, we had a great social life at school. We were in the popular cliques, girls loved us, and we were good at sports. It was all a good distraction and part of the reason I enjoyed escaping to school.

I stopped enjoying it my junior year when Dad got another DUI and all the cars in my family, because they were in his name, had to drive around with "whiskey" plates. In Minnesota, if you get multiple DUIs, you are required to have special plates on your cars. They're white and they start with a W, hence the "whiskey plate" nickname. They're very visible, and everyone knows what they are. It's a form of public humiliation that sticks out like a sore thumb, and I wore that sore thumb every day I drove to school starting my junior year. All of my friends, my friends' parents, my teachers, they all saw it and they all knew. My mom and brother wore the same badge of humiliation on their cars. At this point, my parents were officially separated and living in different homes, but we still had to have the plates on our cars. I hated it.

One day in calculus, one of the senior football players asked me in front of the whole class why I was driving around with whiskey plates. I don't know why he did that, whether he was trying to embarrass me or if he was asking genuinely, but it definitely made me feel humiliated. I didn't answer. The only thing I could do was ignore the public humiliation as best I could. I had no choice but to do that or become a little "poor me" crybaby and fret about it.

I never let it affect me in front of anyone, but on the ride home from football practice that day, I remember praying to God to take my dad out of our life. Make him go away. Make my mom stop crying, make the terrible feelings for my brothers and me go away.

I channeled all of this negative energy onto the football field. It was an exciting year for the team, going to the semi-finals at state for the first time in over a decade, and I had a good enough year that my teammates voted me as one of the team captains the next season.

In one of the last games that year, in October, my dad was in the stands. He'd missed most of the season because he was in rehab. I was proud of him at the time for doing that, seemingly wanting to change his habits.

At the game, we were playing our rivals and losing just after half time. It was the playoffs, so if we lost, the season was over, and it was not looking good. In the third quarter, we took the lead after I intercepted a pass and returned it for a touchdown. On the very next play after the kickoff, I intercepted another pass. We won the game and moved on to win another game and play in the Metrodome. I was on cloud nine. All of my friends loved me, my team loved me, thousands of people cheered for me, and on the bus ride home, I got a text from my dad saying, "I'm so proud of you, son. I love you!"

That's the last sober thing I remember my dad saying to me. About two months later on Christmas Eve, God would answer my prayer. Just not in the way I ever expected.

CHAPTER 3

GRANDMA AND I PARKED IN FRONT of THE BAXTER POLICE station. My heart began to race seeing the cop cars and thinking about two days before, when I was sitting in the back of one. We walked inside where the investigator, a man I recognized from church, greeted us at the door and brought us into a pictureless room. He was holding a manila folder.

"I will be right back. Do you guys want some coffee or water or anything at all?" We shook our heads, and he walked out.

I sat next to Grandma, waiting for the man to come back so I could tell him the details of Christmas Eve. I knew it would be easy to tell him the story because it had been replaying in my head on a loop for two days straight. I felt calm with Grandma there. A constant pillar in my life, someone I knew I could go to. That's why she was the first one I had called that night.

My grandma is the best storyteller I've ever met. My favorite is her story of Kill You, the widowed witch who'd lived just down the road from the Legg family farm when my grandma was a kid. When Grandma was six, her father convinced her and her brother Jim, seven at the time, that Kill You had murdered five of her husbands, and that they both needed to stay away from Kill You's farm no matter what. It was dangerous over there.

With that terrifying education about the dangers of Kill You ingrained in my grandma's head, it only sparked curiosity and a sense of adventure. My great-grandfather could have told them that certain death awaited, and it would have only sparked more curiosity. Fearless, as most kids that age are, not yet fully conditioned to letting fear drive their decisions.

"We should go to her house," Jim said.

"Let's steal some crackers from Kill You," Grandma said, and they were off.

Legend has it that Jim was reaching for the crackers in Kill You's kitchen when my grandma clumsily kicked over a mop bucket, making a crash and causing Kill You to rise from her midday slumber in a rage so deep that the entire town of Forest River, North Dakota could feel the seismic shift. Before Grandma and Jim slammed the door behind them, they saw Kill You grab a hatchet. They were no longer fearless kids, and the three of them were off to the races.

The story always ends with my grandma and Jim running for their lives from Kill You across the field where their father and grandfather were bailing hay, Kill You running after them with the hatchet, and their father yelling, "Run, you little sons a bitches, run! I told you! Run!"

How did the chase end? I have no idea. I never ask that part when she tells it. The story as she tells it is perfect to me, and any more details might ruin it.

Did Kill You exist? Who knows. My great-grandfather probably told Grandma that Kill You would get her so that Grandma
and Uncle Jim wouldn't go over there, for one reason or another.
Maybe he wanted them to stay off the road, maybe there were
dangerous animals over there, or maybe Kill You really was a
man-murdering Feminazi ahead of her time who was angry at
the Patriarchy. I don't know, but parents use fear and try to scare
us into doing things all the time, more often than not for our
own safety and well-being.

I think what is important about this tale is that no matter
how many times we learn something and are told how things
are in the world, we won't fully understand until we find out for
ourselves. We must experience the senses of a situation so we
fully grasp it. Out of stubbornness, curiosity, ignorance—I don't
know why we do it. I think it's different for everyone, but all of
us ignore warning signs and information to seek out the truth
with our own eyes, or to hold on to hope where there is none.
Sometimes as we experience new truths, the loss of innocence
is our own doing. Other times, the Kill You villains come and
de-veil us when we are least expecting it or least willing to face
reality. Fear is born. Fear then takes over.

Books and teachers can't teach you a thing about any of this.
You need to feel it to know it.

I sat with Grandma, waiting. I thought about how scared I
was that night. How scared I was for the future now.

2011

I joined the military because I couldn't afford college, and anyone taking out student loans can't afford it either, but that's what I did for a full year.

I had no business going to college in the first place, not because I wasn't smart enough to do well—I earned a 3.2 GPA my freshman year with a 3.8 in high school—but because I couldn't buy into the college system from the very start. I could not (and still can't) understand why they wanted me to pay $80–$100K for a degree that didn't guarantee me a job. I also couldn't understand why half of that money is spent on taking mandatory liberal arts classes like Women's Studies and Feminism in America. I actually got into a fairly heated argument with my guidance counselor asking why in the hell I needed to take three semesters of Spanish classes. I simply couldn't afford three semesters of something I would likely never utilize. The universities say these classes are to make you a more "well-rounded" person, but that's far from the truth. I know many people with degrees who are awful people and the least well-rounded people I know.

The truth is that college is a scam propped up by government-subsidized loans driving up tuition prices. We are asking eighteen-year-old kids who have never experienced a thing in their life to pick out the career they want for the rest of their lives, then start them off with $100K in the hole as they try to find a job that even pertains to their degree. At eighteen, I was ill-equipped to make this decision when all I knew was girls, football, and baseball. Maybe that's my own fault, or maybe I was just an eighteen-year-old kid.

I succumbed to peer pressure, and, like most eighteen year olds, I fell for this college scam. It's what my high school teachers and friends all said was the next step, so it's what I thought I was supposed to do, even though I didn't want to. I hated school. I did it only because I had to. Memorize a bunch of information, take the bubble test, forget the information, start memorizing more information. What a stupid system.

During spring semester of my freshman year, just as I was scheduling classes for the summer and fall, the next bill for tuition came. I was $4,000 short.

Welp, I thought, *time to take out more loans.* That's what we are supposed to do, right?

The problem with taking out more loans was that my father was in prison, and my mom had had to file bankruptcy after he went away, still weighed down with her own student debt, and now his debt after they consolidated their loans, while also raising two other teenage boys at home. Cash was sparse. $4,000 at that time would have made us feel very wealthy. I didn't know it yet, but I didn't have a cosigner with good enough credit to take out more debt for my education.

I went to my bank. I couldn't take out any more loans there. I tried getting more federal aid, but it was tapped out to the max. I tried getting state aid and aid through my university, but the only grants left to apply for were for minorities or people with disabilities. My "privilege" struck again.

I knew I could find a few jobs that would cover at least part of the bill, and the cycle would continue until after I was done with college. I'd be scraping pennies and eating ramen all the way through, and then when I was done with school and had to start making payments on the loans, the cycle would continue until the day I died. I'd probably be living under a debt rock for decades. How and why did people voluntarily make themselves debt slaves like this? Right then and there I refused to keep going along with it. That's when I started looking into the military. I knew that I would earn money, get my college paid for, get to travel a bit, and experience things no college could teach me, and also be able to serve my country and be of use to others around me.

That summer, I started talking with a recruiter, and by the spring of 2011, I was leaving for basic training and an experience that would change me forever.

After basic, I stayed in San Antonio for my tech school training to be a medic. Specifically a 4N0X1, or an "Aerospace Medical Technician." The training consisted first of classroom training, where they jam you through an EMT-Basic course. On the civilian side it's a six-month course, but in the military they do it in a month and a half. Although the information isn't overly complex, it's a lot in a little amount of time. After each lesson, you take a test, and if you get under a 70 percent on any of the tests, you are washed back to another class to retake the lesson and the same test. If you wash back three times, you are out of the military. Most of us feared washing back and being humiliated like that, so much so that we studied our asses off day and night. Out of twenty of us who started, only four made it through the EMT basic course without washing back at all, myself included.

After EMT basic training, you learn more basic medical knowledge and start some hands-on training. You learn how to do an IV, about cleaning wounds and taking care of patients with mental illnesses like PTSD. Virtually nobody gets washed back in this portion of the training. This lasted about two months, and after this training, you are assigned to a medical facility to do hands-on training with real patients.

I was excited for this part. I knew that the only way to learn more was by doing. I had learned everything I could from the books.

At the time, I didn't know my first day of on-the-job training would teach me more than the previous four months combined.

I was assigned to the emergency room at Fort Sam Houston. It is a trauma center, and San Antonio has a huge population, so the place stays busy 24/7. When I walked in, I saw the ER in full swing. A man in a biker suit was rolled in on a gurney, his motorcycle helmet still on and a giant road rash visible on the left side of his body. I watched through the window as the trauma team went to work. They assessed the man, stabilized his neck, found out what bones were broken, where he was bleeding from, and got him hooked up to fluids. Once they knew he was stable and had his life-threatening wounds tended to, the emergency response ended and the man was wheeled to another room to get further care. All of this happened in the span of just a few minutes. It was a remarkable thing to see so many people working together efficiently to take care of this man.

I was assigned to an Army medic. Sergeant Johnson was his name, and I was to shadow him.

"Just follow me around. I'll teach you when I can, but today, for the most part, we are just going to be doing triage," he said. He was a nice guy, but you could tell having a trainee around wasn't necessarily a joy to him. I'd probably been his hundredth trainee, and a week from then, he'd have another new trainee. Sergeant

Johnson had been in the Army for almost ten years and had been deployed twice. As a trainee just learning, hearing about deployment only piqued my curiosity, and I wanted to pick his brain as much as I could, in case I ever found myself in that situation.

Like a dumbass, one of the first things I asked was, "So what are some of the craziest injuries you've treated here and when you were deployed?"

He kind of got a smirk as he thought about it, probably laughing at my overeagerness to hear about the horrors of medicine. He deflected by saying, "I've treated just about everything man, here and deployed. Maybe before you leave, I'll remember some things to tell you. First we have to talk about triage and what we do up here at Fort Sam."

For the following few hours I learned about triage at the ER on Fort Sam Houston. There were only so many beds in the ER, and even though it was a bigger unit than most trauma centers, they had to prioritize who was seen and try to weed out those who didn't need to take up a bed, which was a lot of people who walked through the door. As I would come to find out quickly, even in the military, many patients came in seeking drugs. Others came in with a sniffle that didn't need the ER's attention, but hey, it was free to them, so who cared? That is what we did up front by the waiting room that day, trying to sort through and triage patients as they came in from most urgent to least urgent. Those who had possible broken bones or things like chest pain got seen before the others.

As I sat there in the triage by the ER waiting room with Sergeant Johnson, I saw a kid, about three years old, running away from his mom as they were leaving the hospital.

"Jamal!" she said. The mom was wearing an Army uniform and pushing another baby in a stroller. She had probably been in the army for at most two years, judging by her E3 rank. "Jamal, if you keep running away someone is going to steal you away. You need to stop doing that!" She grabbed his hand and pulled him out the door as she pushed the stroller with the other hand. I watched them leave and didn't think anything of it.

We started evaluating the next patient in triage. She was in for an ankle sprain, nothing terribly urgent, but I was asking her the questions on the questionnaire like Sergeant Johnson had taught me to, and halfway through the questions I heard, "HEY!"

I turned around and saw an airman running into the ER waiting room holding a limp and unconscious child in his arms. His uniform was covered in blood. As the airman handed the child over to Sergeant Johnson, I saw that the child was Jamal, the same kid getting yelled at by his mom five minutes prior.

Sergeant Johnson sprinted Jamal back to the trauma center.

As Sergeant Johnson disappeared, a team of people burst into the ER waiting room from the parking lot rolling a gurney. On the gurney was a man in his eighties. As they wheeled him by me, I saw the man reaching toward the sky. "Darla! Darla! My wife!" he was crying, as if he was talking to someone above him.

I followed them back to the trauma rooms. This trauma response was not like it was with the guy in the biker helmet. Instead, the place was packed with people and buzzing with full-bird colonels who weren't there before and a real-life general, the first general I had ever seen up close in my military career. There had to be at least one hundred people in the ER. Nurses were wheeling in bags of blood and everyone else not involved in treating the two patients stood by pressed against the walls watching and holding their breath. I remained outside the room where they worked on the boy. So many people were working

on him that I couldn't see him on the table. I stood next to an
army captain. She asked me if I saw them come in. I nodded and
said, "Yes ma'am." The old man was getting worked on through
the window behind me in the second trauma bay.

I can't tell you how long the whole thing lasted, but eventually it ended.

Just a few minutes after they stopped working on the boy,
the mother was brought into the ER. In my thirty-plus years of
life I've only felt time stop twice, and this was one of them. The
place of a hundred people who had been buzzing like a beehive so
loud you couldn't hear yourself think was now still. Not a single
sound. Every eye was on the dead boy's mom.

She had her hand on her mouth trying to hold it all in.
She took three steps like she was wearing cement-filled shoes,
and I can still hear the sound of her three steps slowly hitting
the tile *clop...clop...CLOP*. On the third step, she collapsed to her
knees and let out the loudest and saddest wail I have ever heard.
"Whyyyyyyy?!" She cried on the ground in the middle of the ER
as one hundred people watched. Most crying with her.

The old man died a few days later. He had been driving his car
in the parking lot and had a stroke. In his delirium he hit the gas,
and Jamal wasn't able to move out of the way.

In one of the city's largest trauma centers, patients who
needed care did not stop coming. There wasn't time to continue
to cry with this mom; others needed help. Quickly, other patients
came and the docs and medics went back to work. They had to—
people needed them.

I was back in the front with Sergeant Johnson at triage taking care of patients. He was shaken, visibly. Blood all over his
scrubs still.

"You wanted to know some of the craziest things I've seen?" he said. "Well, there you go."

Sitting with Grandma still waiting for the investigator, I replayed the night in my head for the 500th time in two days. I looked at Grandma and thought about sitting in the back of that cop car with Beau. Beau and I had sat and watched as five police cars and two ambulances waited outside of our house. Staring into our house where the Christmas tree shined bright, waiting to see if Mom was okay. Waiting to see if Devin was okay. I had my cell phone and I called my grandma.

"Hello," Grandma said.

"Grandma... Dad hurt mom," I said. I didn't know how else to say it.

There was a second of silence. "...What?! Why? WHY?! Oh my god!"

I had to stay calm and try to keep Grandma calm. "Grandma, I need you right now. Please stay calm. I don't know what to do."

"We are on our way," she said.

It's 180 miles from Thief River Falls. The trip usually took three hours. That night, my grandma, aunt, and uncle made it in two.

I looked at Grandma and could hear the "Why" from that night.

It's something I was desperately trying to figure out too.

CHAPTER 4

IT WAS THE FALL of 1989 AND MY MOM WAS EIGHTEEN YEARS old. She was home visiting the family farm in Thief River Falls, Minnesota standing in the kitchen with my grandma. My father was in the living room speaking with my grandpa for the first time.

My parents had just started dating. Dad was from Brainerd, which was about three hours south. Mom had moved to Brainerd to attend community college to be a travel agent, and shortly after starting her classes, she met Dad at a party. A few months later they were sitting in Thief River Falls at the family farm.

Soaking wet, Mom was about one hundred pounds, and from across the counter Grandma noticed an abnormal bump in Mom's figure.

"Tricia, are you pregnant?" Grandma asked.

"What? No mom!" she snapped.

My parents left the farm that weekend and drove back to Brainerd.

A few weeks later was Thanksgiving. Mom didn't make it back to the farm for the holiday, but she called during dinner when everyone was over feasting.

Grandma answered the phone.

"Mom?" my mom said with a quivering voice. Grandma could hear the tears through the phone.

"Tricia? What's wrong?" Grandma asked.

"Nothing. I will call back when everyone is gone; I don't want to interrupt everyone's dinner," she said and quickly hung up.

Back at the Thanksgiving party, Grandma leaned over to Grandpa at the dinner table. "Your daughter just called crying."

That evening after everyone left, Grandma called my mom back. "Tricia, why were you crying earlier?"

"Remember a few weeks ago when you asked me if I was pregnant?" she asked. "Well, I am."

After the call, Grandma went out to the shop where Grandpa was cleaning up. "You know what your daughter just told me? She's pregnant. Your daughter is pregnant!"

"With that guy she brought home a few weeks ago?" he asked.

"Yep. That guy," Grandma said. Neither had had the best first impression of my dad from their visit.

Grandpa walked over to the phone and called my mom right away. When she answered, Grandpa asked, "Do you want a crib or a cradle?"

That was it. Mom was terrified to hear what her parents were going to say and do at the news of her being pregnant before being married. Instead of being reprimanded, instead of worrying about what the rest of the community would think, instead of pushing her to get an abortion, my grandfather was there with unwavering and unconditional love.

He handcrafted a crib, and on May 12th, 1990, I was born. On June 21st, Mom turned nineteen, and on June 23rd Mom and Dad got married. Almost a year later, on July 30th, 1991, Devin (a.k.a. "Deev") was born. We were just a few months short of being Irish twins. Barely old enough to have a legal drink, my parents had two kids and no money. It wasn't a perfect start, but in the early nineties our family was bursting onto the Northern Minnesota scene.

Every once in a while I think about how in the hell my parents managed two babies at their age. As I write this, I'm thirty-two and have one child who isn't even one year old, and some days I feel stressed out and ill equipped to give our child what she needs and deserves. How will I provide what my daughter needs? How will I get her as many opportunities as possible? How will I raise a good person when I still barely know the answers to all of this for myself? My parents had to try and figure all of this out at twenty-one with *two* kids? I can't imagine.

One thing I know for certain is that my mom had a rock solid support system from her family and friends. Specifically my grandma and grandpa, as well as my mom's two older brothers, Brent and Tron. Devin and I were at the farm with our grandparents all the time. We loved it there. Grandpa was my hero, and in my eyes he was larger than life. He drove giant tractors and raised animals, and in the winter he worked at Arctic Cat, the coolest place I knew of at the time. He carried himself with a strength of character that no other man I knew did. People respected him. He was without question the rock of the family.

Although Grandpa supported Mom and her new family, he kept my dad at arm's length. He didn't fully trust him yet. Grandma told me once, after a few glasses of wine, that when Mom was about to walk down the aisle to marry Dad, Mom was crying. Grandpa allegedly told my mom before he walked her down the aisle, "You don't have to do this if you don't want to."

She did walk down the aisle, and Grandpa was right there to walk with her and support her decision, even if he thought maybe it wasn't the right one.

At the time, Grandpa was undoubtedly a part of my mom's inner circle, a part of the theory of Dunbar's number. Dunbar's theory states that we can manage only so many relationships in our lives. We all have some form of inner circle, generally about five people, who we have our deepest relationships with. The theory goes on to say that, in total, at one time we can manage about 150 relationships, with most of those being people we may talk to only once a year. If you think about it, this makes sense. We only have so much time in a day—it's literally impossible to develop and manage more than a handful of strong relationships. This makes today's social media–driven world seem kind of silly and even more superficial. Why are we friends on Facebook with the person we knew fifteen years ago from high school when we will never talk to them again? We see their posts pop up on our feeds and we waste time comparing our lives to theirs when our relationship with them is about as shallow as it gets? Why don't we prioritize our real relationships and strengthen our inner circles? I ask myself this all the time, and I understand how easy it is to lose sight of. One day, loss and grief will come into our lives, and our fake 500 Facebook friends may leave a "thoughts and prayers" comment, but they won't be the ones with you in the hospital or at the gravesite. Why do we waste our time?

Another person in Mom's inner circle was one of her best friends, Dana. Dana and my mom grew up together in Thief River Falls and dreamed of running away from their small town one day to make it big somewhere. In the state's only county without a lake, Pennington County, there's not much else to do but dream big. It's that or drink, and there's plenty of people already doing that. Mom and Dana used to ride bikes ten miles one way on the gravel roads just to hang out and plan their great escape. Instead of escaping to the big city, at almost the same time in 1989, Dana got pregnant with her daughter, Kayla. For the next few years, Mom and Dana were calling each other, swapping tips about what to do when babies have hand, foot, and mouth and which stores had the best coupons for diapers and baby food.

When I think about how hard it must have been for Mom—a kid herself raising two kids—I also think about the people she had in her life who were doing it all with her. I know she would go through those hard times again if it meant they would be right there by her side again.

Then you have my mom's two older brothers who gave her hell growing up. One of my favorite brotherly love stories is when it was Mom's first day of kindergarten in the late seventies, which would have put my uncles in about fifth and sixth grade. Mom was wearing a pretty dress and was excited for her first day when, right before they left, her brother Brent grabbed her head, pushed it down, and farted on her. The stench was so bad that my mom puked all over her brand new dress and was late for her first day of kindergarten. As mean as that might seem, my uncles would have murdered anyone who laid a finger on their little sister.

As Mom was dealing with Devin and me, my uncle Tron (her oldest brother) had two kids around our age, Jenny and Aaron, and Brent had three kids, Garrett, Kyle, and Chelsey, all around our age too. Beau would be the last to join us in 1996. Eight grand-kids running around the farm and money was tight for everyone. Instead of following the travel agent path, Mom began working in nursing as an LPN. Dad worked at the jail and eventually became a dispatcher. Tron worked construction, and his wife, Kelly, was a school lunch lady. Brent was a plumbing apprentice and his wife, Janice, worked at one of the local bars. When I say money was tight, I mean my uncle Brent used to poach deer, cut it up, and disperse it to everyone to help out on the grocery bills. For a few years, Mom used food stamps to get us by while she was in school. We had no idea we were poor. We had food at every meal and gifts on our birthdays and holidays. As far as I knew, we were living the dream.

One of my favorite stories from that time is when Mom had all three of us boys at the grocery store. I was seven, Devin six, and Beau around one. Beau was in the little seat that comes on shopping carts and Devin and I were running around like little lunatics. Mom had a cart full of groceries, and while mom was pushing, I kept jumping onto it and standing on the side.

"Get down from there, you're going to get hurt," she repeated.

Mom stopped the cart and turned with her coupon book to look at the shelves, and, as she did, I jumped on the side again, only Mom wasn't holding onto the cart anymore to stop it from tipping over on me. The cart full of groceries—and Beau in the seat—fell on top of me. We both started bawling, groceries scattered the cereal aisle like a bomb went off and mom was so embarrassed that she grabbed us off the floor and left. I don't know what we ate that night, but I know we didn't get groceries for at least a few days, and we definitely did not go with her to get them.

In 1996, when Beau was born, we were still in Thief River Falls, surrounded by our extended family. You could throw a rock in any direction and hit another family member's house.

Not long after he was born our family moved about four hours away to a little town called Saginaw near Duluth. Although we moved away from all of our extended family and the family farm, our most beloved place, we moved closer to Mom's friend Dana and her husband, Joe, who had moved there a few years earlier. We traded our cousins for Dana's kids. Kayla was my age, Taylor was a year younger than Devin, and Noah was born within a few months of Beau.

We were with Dana's family all the time, who were in an almost identical situation as my parents. Three kids and struggling to make ends meet. Our parents always got creative, entertaining us and keeping us busy without spending a lot of money. In the winters there was endless amounts of time spent out in the snow, and once it got dark at 4 p.m., we would have movie marathons where we would all go pick out a movie at the video rental store (or the library). Then we'd make a giant blanket bed in the living room and watch the movies we picked out and eat popcorn and candy. We were entertained for the weekend for just a few dollars. In the summers we were always camping. Mom and Dana didn't make it to New York City or even Minneapolis to live out the big city dream. Instead they were living another dream, each raising three kids and doing it together down the road from each other in Duluth.

Although we didn't have a giant house or fancy cars, my family taught us kids how important the relationships are in our lives. To be there for each other, no matter what. We were poor as hell, but for the most part in the early nineties, things seemed to be pretty good and everyone seemed happy. Priorities weren't the *things* around us, they were each other. I always look back on these times when I need to remind myself how and what to prioritize.

Mom always had the people in her life first, and, as hard as her situation was, being a young mom in an abusive marriage, she was making it work. I'm convinced it's because she put people first in her life. But things were about to get much harder for her, and fast.

It was the summer of 1997. I had just turned seven and we were in the heart of camping season. By seven, I was a seasoned camper with dozens of trips under my belt. As much as I hated sleeping in a tent, I loved going fishing and being outside with my cousins, and on this trip Kayla and Taylor were going to be there with all of us. I knew it was going to be a blast. With the extra two people, I thought we might even be able to fill up a hundred jars of fireflies. We were going to Norway Beach near Bemidji and meeting the rest of our family from Thief River Falls there.

We were running late as we left our house. We were meeting Dana, Joe, and the kids at a gas station just outside of town. The gas station was located on a corner, so there were pumps on both sides of the store. We pulled into the one side, my dad parking in front of a gas pump to fill up. While he started pumping, he noticed a lot of commotion coming from the other side. People stood and watched from afar. A few police cars arrived with their lights on, and after a few minutes, there was even a news helicopter circling above.

Dad left the gas pump and walked over to see what was going on. He was gone for about a minute, and, I can remember like it was yesterday, Dad turning the corner and walking back toward our car. His face was pale as he walked up to the passenger door and said, "Trish, it's Dana and Joe." Mom got out of the car, and after she turned the corner of the store to where the scene of the car accident was, I don't remember seeing her again for a few days.

Multiple helicopters now circled above. Dad contacted our babysitter, and she came with her mom and got us. As we were leaving the gas station with them I saw the scene of the car crash. There was a white sheet covering the front passenger seat and the person in it.

Joe had been turning into the gas station. He thought he had time to turn before the oncoming car passed, but he didn't, and the front side passenger door was hit square.

Mom rode to the hospital in the ambulance with the two girls, and Joe was rushed in another ambulance.

A piece of my mom died that day with Dana. This was one of my mom's closest friends and someone in her inner circle. A relationship that she'd built over decades, filled with good and bad experiences, filled with memories. Filled with love. Gone in the snap of a finger. No more midnight phone calls. No more camping trips. Nothing. It was the saddest I'd ever seen someone in my seven years of life. As for the girls, their hearts were forever shattered that day. We would see them occasionally after the accident, usually on birthdays and grad parties, but we slowly grew apart. Every year, there are pictures of Dana's beautiful smile on social media, and the girls post pictures of visiting her gravesite. I had no grasp of the concepts of loss and grief, but this was my first experience with it. Within a year, we would see loss and grief again.

For a few years, we knew Grandpa was sick. When he was diagnosed with cancer, he was treated, and after about a year, he was in remission. A year after Dana's death, Grandpa's cancer came back, this time in his pancreas, a spot that is about 95 percent fatal. It was the morning of November 6th, 1998 and we were packing up the car getting ready to head to Thief River Falls for deer hunting opener when Mom got the phone call. She and Dad sat us on the couch and told us Grandpa had died that morning. We all sobbed together for what seemed like an hour. My hero was gone. I couldn't believe it.

Just gone forever? That's it? I had the hardest time trying to make sense of it all. *Why? Why did he have to go? He wasn't even old. Why?* I said it over and over.

Grandpa was on the farm when he died. I think everyone besides us kids knew the severity of his situation, so they'd put a hospital bed for him in the living room so he could look out the big window of the farmhouse. He died right there in the place that he'd built with his bare hands. My uncle Brent was in the room with him when he died early that morning and says he heard Grandpa say, "I'm not ready yet."

When Grandpa died he left a will that gave each of us grand-kids one of his guns and split up his farmland between Brent, Tron, Grandma, and my mom. One of my favorite places on the farm was the basement where Grandpa had a giant board of lit-tle trinkets he'd found over the years. There were dozens of old arrowheads, cool rocks, old shell casings, and even a gun he'd found. The weekend he died, when I was down there looking at his collection, I found a gray metal box with his name on it. It was about five inches wide, eight inches long, and three inches deep. Inside was an old wallet with some of his expired ID cards and old pictures. I asked my grandma if I could keep it, and she said absolutely. From that day forward, it became my "important things only" box. Anything incredibly important to me went in the box, and I kept it under my bed or in my closet next to my bed, so I could still see it when I walked into my room. I would see it every day, see his name, and be reminded of him. It was my way to never forget my hero.

Every person reading this and every person who will ever exist will experience loss and grief at some point. Maybe you already have. When we lose people in our inner circle it leaves a giant hole. Sometimes a hole that is never fully repairable. This is a person you may have called for advice or called to celebrate your promotion or called when you needed help. All of a sudden they are just gone and you have to find a new person or place to turn to. I've seen people turn to drugs, alcohol, and just let go when these tragedies happen. They lose someone and they just give up. I'm not saying that's a good thing, but I understand it. Within a one-year span, my mom lost two of the closest people in her life. Her best friend and her father. Two pillars in my mom's life gone forever. Her inner circle shattered.

I remember Mom crying a lot, but the thing that kept her going was she knew she was a pillar in other people's lives. In our lives. She had to be strong too. And she was. She worked her ass off and became the only LPN hired when the new surgery center was opened in the town we eventually moved to, Brainerd. While we were preteens and busier than hell with baseball and friends, my mom went back to school to become an RN, and today, she is the nurse manager and one of two original people left at the surgery center from when it first opened. She exudes strength, even amidst the chaos. She kept working hard, and having that to look up to was the greatest gift any of us could have received.

Mom showed us that there is life after tragedy and grief. Even while lying in a hospital bed after getting beat to within an inch of her life, she didn't ever stop and sulk or say, "Poor me."

Being the best you and the strongest you is the most important thing you can do for the people in your life. We are all a pillar in other people's lives, and they need us. We can mourn for years and years and just abandon anything of meaning in this life or we can forge ahead. It took me a long time to see and understand this.

As I said, my grandparents were not the biggest fans of my dad. They thought he was arrogant and cocky, but they ignored the red flags as best they could and supported Mom, because my mom wanted to try and make it work for her kids. My grandpa taught my dad how to hunt and fish and let him use the farm shop to work on vehicles and whatever other projects he had going on. Looking back, it's funny how life presents us with the foreshadowing of fate, if you believe in that. I think it's very easy to cherry pick dots to connect in anything we want to connect—confirmation bias if you want to call it that—and I'm generally a huge skeptic. But a few dots and events from that time in our lives feel hard not to connect.

In the spring of 1998, before Grandpa got really sick, there was a benefit in town to help him and my grandma with the costs of treatment and travel. The morning before the benefit, my cousins and I spent the day on the farm. Usually you could find us outside shooting BB guns or playing hide and seek, but on that day, we were taking turns riding the go-cart our grandpa had bought for all of us grandkids. It had become the most prized toy on the farm. It wasn't any faster than a golf cart—it had a roll cage on it and was super low to the ground. It was a pretty safe machine, even for a bunch of kids. Plus, if we got caught without helmets on, we were grounded from the go-cart for the weekend, even though the helmets were open faced, with no visor or protection around your jawline, like a baseball batting helmet. Still, it was a rule none of us wanted to break.

That morning, Devin had the go-cart out by himself, ripping around the farm's dirt road circle driveway and back in the walking paths in the trees.

The rest of us felt that Devin was hogging the go-cart for too long, and after a while, my cousin Aaron and I took a walk trying to find out where he was. He hadn't passed by us on the circle driveway for about ten minutes. Unless he was driving toward the Canadian border, we should have seen him drive by.

We followed the hum of the small engine, and as we walked toward the sound, it got louder, and so did Devin's scream.

Louder and louder until it sounded like Devin was being tortured, when all of a sudden Devin rounded the corner, the scream deafening. When I saw him, his face was covered in blood. Like a scene from *Carrie*, his face was jacked up. He ran right past us and up to the farmhouse, screaming the whole way.

Aaron and I walked farther to where we found the go-cart still running, as if nothing had happened. We grabbed some helmets and started riding, leaving our parents to mend the broken Devin.

It turns out Devin had rolled the go-cart, and when he did, he hit his face on the steering wheel, breaking his nose. He was so scared of getting in trouble that he'd made sure to roll the go-cart back upright, face gushing blood as he did, before he went inside to get help.

He didn't want to go to the benefit because of how he looked, but Devin showed up that night looking like Mike Tyson squared him up, and half the town of about 8,000 people saw his broken schnoz.

A year and half later, in 1999, we were in Thief River Falls a lot. After Grandpa died we visited much more than we used to, and while we were there on the weekends that year, my dad decided to build his own go-cart, welding the frame himself and doing it around an old snowmobile engine. He did so while putting down a twelve pack here and there... Welding and drinking. Not a good idea.

When it came time to test drive his monster, things went exactly as you would expect them to go. On the day of the test ride, Dad took the go-cart out toward the highway, about a half mile long dirt road, and as he drove away from us, you could see something wasn't right. He swerved and nearly went into the ditch, going on two wheels multiple times and doing so at a very high speed. He finally got it under control and came to a stop. We ran the half mile down the dirt road where he parked to see what was going on. He said "the throttle was sticking." This should have been his signal to put the death trap in neutral and have us push it back to the shop, but he got in and decided to give it another ride, which proved to be a terrible decision, and almost fatal.

We were standing on the dirt road looking toward the farm. The driveway is a simple setup—you take a right off the half-mile dirt road from the paved highway and you are on the start of the farm's circle driveway. As you drive around the circle counter clockwise, the farmhouse is on your left in the middle of the circle, and as you pass the house, you get back toward the

farm equipment. Four grain bins, a giant pole shed full of tractors, and the entrance to the cow pasture, among various other
pieces of equipment sitting along the circle, depending on the
time of the year.

Dad sped off from where we were standing going full speed.
He looked like a drag racer taking off toward the farmhouse.
He took the right into the circle driveway and was headed right
toward the farm equipment, full speed.

My heart started to race as I knew something wasn't right. He
was about 150 yards from sure death when, all of a sudden, the
machine swerved onto two wheels and somersaulted through
the air in a cloud of dirt road dust. The go-cart flipped and rolled
at least four or five times. Pieces of metal and a blue helmet flying
in all directions. I thought for sure I had just watched my dad die.

"Dad!" I yelled, running toward the cloud of dust. When the
cloud settled Dad laid in a heap in his blue shirt torn to shreds,
helmet gone, and most of the life in him gone too.

"H-help," he let out.

I ran inside and got Mom and my uncle. "Dad just crashed the
go-cart, and he's hurt!"

They rushed outside, and instead of waiting for an ambulance, they loaded him up into a truck and sped off to town with
the flashers on. When it was all said and done, he suffered a handful of broken ribs, a punctured lung, and a broken clavicle. It was
a miracle that he escaped with his life.

Over the next few months, while Dad recovered from his
accident, I began to notice him acting funny, like he was drunk,
but I knew he wasn't drinking. It only ever happened when he
took his "pain medicine."

The part of the story that gets weird for me is the part where my brothers and I stayed at the farm with my grandma as they rushed Dad to the hospital.

At the time, Beau was around three and a half. Devin, Beau, Grandma, and I were all sitting in the living room looking out at the driveway. From that view, you can see where the crash began. As we sat there, Beau looked out the window and said, "Grandma, it's Grandpa."

We all looked at each other, confused.

Grandma asked him, "Grandpa as in your Grandpa Lew?" Lew was my dad's dad and lived three hours away in Brainerd.

"No, it's Grandpa Erv," Beau said, pointing out the window.

"Beau, your grandpa Erv is in heaven. He can't be standing there," Grandma said.

"He's right there, Grandma!" Beau insisted.

I looked at my grandma and Devin.

"Grandma, make him stop!" Devin said.

Grandma took Beau off the couch and set him on the floor. All of us were too scared to look, but I wish I would have.

They say little kids can tap into things that adults can't, and that's the one example I have in my life that makes me think that might be true.

A foreshadowing of fate? Whether it be divine or coincidence, the universe did a great job setting up the years to come.

CHAPTER 5

I was headed back to the police station, still only a few days removed from the incident. We were staying with my uncle Tron and aunt Kelly. They had a small trailer house south of town that we all bunched into until Mom was better and until we had a new place to move into. Mom was just about to get out of the hospital, and we were supposed to go back to school in a few days after Christmas break was over. Part of me just wanted to leave town and finally move back up to Thief River Falls where we used to live and be near the rest of our family. We'd be by them and we wouldn't have to see everyone at school after all of this. I prayed that maybe most people at school simply wouldn't hear about it.

I was heading back to the police station, by myself this time, because the investigator had my cell phone. They took it that night because they "needed to see the texts my dad was sending that night." So for a few days I didn't have any contact with any of my friends, or anyone for that matter, but I didn't really care.

I didn't want to face anyone, and without having my phone, it made that easier to accomplish.

I arrived at the police station and met the investigator at the door.

"Hey Desmond, how's everything going for you since we last spoke? Come on in, I have your phone just over here."

I followed him inside. He grabbed my phone, which was in a little bag.

"Here you go. We're done with this. Sorry we had to take it from you," he said and handed me the phone, a silver razor.

"You got a few minutes?" he asked me. "I just wanted to ask you a few more questions that I didn't get to ask before."

"Yeah, I don't have anything else going on. We can talk now," I said and followed him into the same office as before.

We sat down at the table, and he had his manila folder.

"Before I get to anything else, how are you and your brothers holding up? If you guys need anything, you let me know. I know I gave you one of these before, but here's my card again with all of my information."

"We're good, I guess. I don't really know what to say to that, to be honest. It all just feels like a dream is the best I can say. It's weird." And it did feel like a dream. The situation was surreal. I kept reliving the whole thing over and over and over again. The pictures kept replaying. I thought about Mom and how she would be after all of this. How Devin would be.

I also may have spoken to my dad for the last time ever, I thought. I didn't ever want to talk to him again. *But that's my dad. My only dad. And now he's gone.* He wasn't dead, but he was gone. Again, surreal.

Nobody prepares you for something like this happening. You see these types of things on the news, but you never plan on your family actually being there. I didn't know how to sort out how I felt, so it was hard to answer his question.

"Well again, if you need me I'm here. I mean that," he said.

"Thanks, I appreciate it."

He opened his manila folder back up. "Obviously, depending on how the court process plays out, your dad is going to likely face some time for what he did. It's important that the information and evidence we collect now is whole so they can best charge him to make the process as smooth and just as possible for everyone. It's innocent until proven guilty for everyone, even though it's pretty obvious what his actions were the other night. Now the remaining questions are: Why? Where was his head? I'm sure you've been wondering all that yourself."

I nodded, sitting there waiting for the questions.

"That night with the other investigator, you told him you knew this was going to happen, that you even told your mom that if you guys went back to the house that he was going to come and possibly hurt someone. How did you know that? What made you believe that he could do such a thing?"

I sat and thought for a minute. Trying to figure out where to begin.

DECEMBER 24TH, 2007

We were on our way back from Thief River Falls. We were staying up at my grandma's trailer house for the weekend celebrating Christmas with her and our other family members. Her house was in a nice trailer park, and I enjoyed going up there. Grandma's trailer park was nicer than the one we lived at when we first moved to Brainerd. Ours had some great people in it, but also the kinds of people who threw their wife's clothes out into the middle of the street because she'd smoked too many cigarettes from the communal pack of darts and didn't have money for three days to buy more, as well as people who had been living off disability for a decade when they did not, in fact, have any back problems. Just a few more shysters and shady characters in our park than my grandma's. After Grandpa died, the three of us boys each spent a week alone with Grandma in the summers. It was always a great escape for a week, usually after baseball and right before football started. Just hanging out at the shoe store Grandma worked at and then going to hang out with my cousins, then coming home to some delicious Grandma-made dinner.

That Christmas Eve, once we got home from Thief River, we were supposed to go to our dad's apartment, but we were running a little bit behind. We'd be about an hour late, and he wasn't happy about it.

I was sitting in the back seat on the drive home, and by his texts, I could tell he was pretty pissed off. Stuff like, "Your mom is just as screwed up as I am, but I'm the bad guy in all this?" He had this idea that Mom was trying to keep us from him, which wasn't the case at all. I was seventeen, Devin was sixteen. Old enough to see through any sort of manipulation going on. We'd been around long enough and seen these cycles play out enough to know how he operated.

Still, as I read his texts I felt the pit in my stomach growing. Just two months earlier, Dad had been finishing up rehab at Hazelden, a world-renowned recovery center, which I was proud of him for doing, but I knew just by reading his texts that he was probably drinking or under some sort of influence. I had developed a sort of sixth sense with my dad and his personality shifts. I absolutely hated him when he was drinking. *Hated* him. I knew what could happen when he drank, and every time he did, I was on edge. Literally lying in my bed and not sleeping until I knew he had passed out. He would go through phases of drinking and not drinking. Then after his go-cart accident, he started getting his prescriptions.

Once, when I was about twelve, he stopped drinking for a few months and suddenly, one evening, started again. For some reason, that time I had the courage to confront him about it. He was drinking Hamm's. It's weird how I know that detail, but I can see him right now holding the Hamm's can, with the empties sitting on the garage tool bench.

"Dad, are you going to keep drinking much longer?"

He threw his beer.

"Your mom told you to ask me that?"

Mom hadn't said a word to me. She didn't need to. I knew enough on my own to hate his drinking. Thinking Mom had been saying things to me, he got mad at her and the shouting match began.

Driving back to Brainerd on Christmas Eve in 2007, I felt that exact same pit in my stomach from when I was a kid, knowing he was at his apartment waiting for us. Alone, drinking, and pissed off.

My parents at the time were split up and in the middle of finalizing a divorce. They had been split since earlier that summer. I didn't really know why they were splitting up. They just said it was happening, and I felt huge relief over it. I found out later that *he* wanted the divorce, not my mom.

This wasn't the first time they had split up. In 2004, right before Christmas, we'd just gotten home from Thief River Falls after a long weekend, and my parents had been fighting the whole ride home. When we got home, Dad was walking up the steps, Devin and Beau ahead of him, when he turned to my mom and threw the car keys at her.

Mom grabbed them, got in the van, and said, "I'm leaving! I'm done being treated like this."

I knew the look in Dad's eyes, and it scared the hell out of me. I jumped in the van with Mom. Dad trapped my brothers inside the house, and they were stuck there with him. Before I jumped in the van, Dad said, "Des, come on, let's go open presents while your mom walks out on us."

After that, Mom and I drove to my dad's sister and her husband's house where Mom told them what had happened. Later that evening, my mom, aunt, and uncle went and got Devin and Beau, and for a week, including Christmas, we were at my aunt's. After that, my parents were split up for about four months. Dad lived with a friend, and the three of us boys split time between our mom and dad. It wasn't ideal. I was just entering high school, a freshman at the time, and I was worrying about girlfriends, my friends, sports, my future—then all of a sudden, I had to start trying to figure out where I was staying that night, Mom's or Dad's, and what kind of arguments I'd be tiptoeing around.

I don't blame anyone for getting divorced and am not judging if you've been through one—some people shouldn't be together, and my parents are included in that group—but I feel bad for any kid who lives with divorced parents. Especially if they are hopping from house to house on the weekends. I don't know how to make it not suck for kids in that situation, but the best thing I heard a divorced couple do is they had the kids stay at one house full time, and the parents were the ones who came and went, not the kids. So instead of having the kids go to mom's in one town for three days and then to Dad's a half hour away for three days, the parents came and went every three days to the house. They each had their own room in the house with the kids and shared an apartment with their own rooms as well. I thought that was incredibly thoughtful. Instead of putting the bulk of stress and hassle on their kids, they put it on themselves.

Flash forward to when I was seventeen and my parents had split up the second time. When my parents announced that they were splitting up, Dad rented a two-bedroom apartment about a mile away from where we lived. There was no set in stone expectation for Devin and I to be splitting time at his place, but Dad didn't like it when we didn't come over enough. At the time, I had a seventeen-year-old's social life: I had baseball every day until August when I started football, and I also worked a full-time job in the summer. I was barely at our regular home as it was, and to try and get over to a second home, on top of everything, was hard. Not to mention our dad's had one extra bed in it, and there were three of us boys. Beau was the only one who split time between our parents regularly.

After a while, Dad started coming over for dinner at our mom's. It felt weird, acting like everything was normal when it wasn't, and I didn't want to sit there any more pretending it was. I told Mom how I felt about him coming over, and when she relayed that message to Dad, he didn't like it. This only added to his ideation that Mom was manipulating us to push him away.

That Christmas Eve drive home in 2007 I was thinking about all of this as Dad texted me. We finally got home to Mom's from Thief River, and we started getting ready for our dad's by grabbing his presents and our clothes to spend the next few nights at his apartment. Dad was still texting me once we got inside, and the pit in my stomach was a solid rock now.

"Mom, I don't want to go over there," I told her.

"You have to. You spent time with me, and now you have to go spend time with him."

Damn it, I thought. I went downstairs to my room and sat on the edge of my bed thinking about the upcoming night. I knew things weren't right. Whenever he was drunk and/or high, he was a monster, and I didn't trust him. Not even a tiny bit.

As I sat there, not wanting to pack, I thought about a time when I was six years old. We lived in Thief River Falls still, not long before we moved to Duluth. Devin and I shared a bedroom, which was a normal thing for us until we moved to the trailer park in 1998, then I got my own room and Devin and Beau shared a room. The house before that, right outside of Morgan Park in Duluth, all three of us boys shared a room. It was tiny, so the trailer house was a nice upgrade. At our home in Thief River, to make our room seem a little bigger, Dad built us bunk beds. It was much cheaper than buying a bunk bed from the store, so a couple two by fours, a few sheets of plywood, and some screws, and Deev and I had our beds and a larger floor space to play. I had the top bunk. It was very sturdy and safe, with a guard rail on the side in case I rolled too far to the edge.

One night, Devin and I went to bed, and in the middle of the night, I rolled over into the railing. The railing prevented me from falling off the edge, but I was snapped awake by a stinging sensation on my back that jolted me awake. I immediately started bawling. Mom rushed in to see what was happening. When she turned on the light, we saw a screw sticking out of the railing, and I had rolled right into it.

Instead of going back to sleep in my own bed, Mom let me lay in her and Dad's bed. Dad was out that night. I laid on Dad's side of the bed, my back still stinging, but eventually I fell asleep.

I was jolted awake once more by the blinding glare of the bedroom light turning on. I looked up and saw Dad standing in the doorway.

"What's this?" he said.

Mom started explaining to him that I'd hurt myself on a screw that he'd forgotten to make sure wasn't poking out when he'd built the beds. As he started getting defensive with her, like it wasn't his fault, I felt underneath me on the bed. It was soaking wet. I had pissed the bed when I'd fallen asleep, something Devin and I both did until we were about seven. Even taking preventative measures like peeing before bed, not drinking anything a few hours before bed, it just happened. Something I thought I was at fault for, but in reality, is something that is out of the control of a six-year-old. Dad was yelling at my mom, trying to defend himself about the screw, when I uncovered myself and he saw the piss. He cut himself off midsentence to turn his attention to me.

"Are you fuckin' serious?" he said, looking at me. He walked around the bed to me, grabbed me by the Ninja Turtles pajama shirt, and raised me up off the bed toward the ceiling. I smelled the beer on his breath. I felt the fear course through me while he assessed the puddle on his side of the bed. Then he threw me up against the dresser. I bashed against it and fell to the floor.

"Stop it!" Mom screamed. I have a vivid image from that night, sitting at the base of the dresser, soaked in piss, sobbing, and reaching up for my mom as she screamed at Dad through her own tears.

I can't describe a feeling worse than powerlessness. Walking around on eggshells, waiting for—and trying to stay out of the way of—the next snap. Then, when the snap comes, just sitting there and riding out the storm, no control, just praying for the least amount of damage possible. At six years old, there's not much you can do against a six-foot-two, 250-pound pissed off drunk man. There's not much you can do when you're a 110-pound woman, either. Now, when I was seventeen, I still didn't feel safe around him, but I was starting to build my own muscle and athletic stature.

As I sat on the bed, thinking about this, I realized that the pit in my stomach was that powerless feeling. My body was hardening itself for the upcoming emotional battle, and although it wasn't all the time, I didn't put a physical battle past him.

I reached under my bed and pulled out Grandpa's gray metal box. In it I still had Grandpa's wallet, which was now full of two-dollar bills that Grandma sent us on the holidays with her cards. There were medals from my sports, family pictures, and some money I had saved up. I wasn't looking for any of that on that night. Instead I grabbed the hunting knife that I kept in there and put it in my pocket.

"So you brought the knife with you because you knew something bad was going to happen," the investigator said.

"Yeah, I wasn't going to be defenseless at his apartment. Something was telling me to grab it and bring it with me. Something wasn't right. I could feel it. I knew it," I said. "I've seen this cycle too many times now. I knew a snap was coming. I just knew that one day when he snapped, he was finally going to go too far. Obviously, I was right, and he did go too far."

The officer nodded. "You don't need to explain yourself to me anymore. After what you've told me I wouldn't have felt safe if I were you either, and you know what? I'm sorry. I wish we could have done something to stop this from happening."

I didn't know what to say to that. *Was there even a way for them to stop something like that?* I thought. He broke the silence.

"All right, well, that's really everything else I had. We shouldn't have to call you back for any more questions. I know you probably don't want to talk about it anymore."

We stood up, and he shook my hand. As we were about to walk to the door, he remembered something.

"Ah, I'm sorry, one more thing. I know you got the knife from under your bed, but where exactly did you get that knife before that?"

NOVEMBER 2001

I sat on a bucket between two birch trees. I held an SKS Rifle in my lap. Snow on the ground and I could see every breath as I peered out into the woods. Waiting.

Crack...

The sound startled me, and my heart began to pound.

Crack...

I raised my rifle as slow as I could, trying to look around me so I wouldn't startle him with any quick movements. I still couldn't see him. My heart pounded faster.

CRACK!

There he was right in front of me...a rabbit.

I lowered my rifle, a wave of disappointment cleansed the adrenaline from my blood. It wasn't the thirty-point buck that I was looking for. At eleven years old, I'd been out hunting with my family almost every year. I loved walking through the woods in a line and trying to flush out the deer to the guys sitting on the road waiting to shoot them. Then, after we shot a deer, the whole group would go back and clean the deer in the shop. I loved it. That was my first year carrying a gun after Devin and I got our gun safety certificates, and I was eager to shoot my first deer.

As I sat on the bucket waiting, Dad and Devin sat about a hundred yards to my back, looking in the other direction. We had the whole area covered, so if there was a deer within a 200-yard radius, we would see him.

We had been sitting there for about an hour and a half, and I knew at some point we'd be leaving to meet up with the rest of the hunting party. I looked back toward Dad and Devin to see if they were headed my way yet.

CRACK!

I whipped my head around and he was standing right there, about thirty yards away.

A buck! My heart pounded harder than ever, and when I raised my rifle I couldn't stop myself from shaking. I locked eyes with him, and he just stood there. I took a deep breath to try and stop myself from shaking and aimed where I knew I was supposed to...*BANG.*

He took one jump and dropped about five feet from where he was standing. A perfect shot.

"I got him! He's down!" I yelled to my dad and Devin. A few minutes later they walked over and the three of us walked up to the deer. I was floating. I was so proud of myself. I just shot a five-point buck. I couldn't wait to show my friends and tell the rest of my family and the hunting party.

"Nice job, buddy! I'm so proud of you!" Dad said. Putting my dad in a good mood and hearing him say stuff like that was always a great day. No snaps and I felt like he truly was proud of me when he said it. It was a great feeling.

"Now we have to clean him. Ready to get your hands dirty?" Dad pulled out a buck knife and for the next twenty minutes he taught me everything I needed to know to clean a deer.

"Killing something is a big deal. Whenever you kill something you have to make sure you don't waste any of the animal. This deer gave its life so we can eat. Never take killing something lightly. Only when you are going to eat it or if your life or someone else's life is in danger. That's it."

We got done cleaning the deer, and before we started dragging it out of the woods, Dad wiped off, folded up, and handed me the hunting knife. "This is yours. Make sure you hold onto it for later when we start processing the rest of him at the farm. And for the next deer you shoot next year!" He gave me a hug, and we began to drag the deer out of the woods.

When we got home from Thief River Falls that weekend, I made sure to wash my new knife and get it as clean as possible. When I was done, I took out Grandpa's gray metal box from under my bed and set the knife in it.

CHAPTER 6

DECEMBER 2011

It was my first Christmas away from my brothers and my mom since 2007, and I was far away. As in halfway around the world away. After my medical training in San Antonio, I was assigned to my first base, Kadena Air Base in Okinawa.

When I'd first gotten the orders, I texted Mom and said, "I got my first base, staying here in San Antonio for the next two years." She was excited, responding, "Awesome, that's only a few hours' flight away!" I'd texted her Texas because I'd confused my orders, which said "Kadena," with "Madina," which was an off-shoot of Lackland in San Antonio. Thinking I was staying in Texas, I was a little bit disappointed. I loved Texas, but I wanted to get out and see more of the world. When I'd told my friends, "Hey guys, I'm staying here in Texas. I got Kadena," they'd looked at me like I was an idiot.

"And you look like your dog died? Bro, I would kill for Japan," my roommate had said.

"Japan?" I'd said.

"Yeah. Bro, you got like, a top three assignment in the entire Air Force."

I started thinking about the upcoming chapter. A whole new culture and adventure, just like I was hoping for. But I'd told Mom Texas...

I immediately called her and told her about my mistake. Knowing that I would be out of the country, about a thirteen-hour time difference, and a $1,500+ plane ticket away, I could tell Mom was disappointed, but she tried to seem excited for me. After training, I returned home on leave for a week, then left Minneapolis for Japan three weeks before Christmas in 2011. When Mom, my stepdad, Brent, and I went to the airport, she cried as they left me at the gate.

When I arrived in Okinawa, the Christmas decorations on base were up, and it felt almost as festive as the states, minus the snow. That was weird to get used to since I always associated Christmas with snow and had never seen a Christmas without it. Even without the cold and winter powder, Christmas parties were planned at the squadrons, and the spirit was in the air. Those first few weeks before Christmas, I settled into my new dorm room and got a feel for the base and the new group of people around me. I had a great feeling about the next two years and was excited about my new temporary home.

The first time it ever happened to me was that first Christmas Eve away from Mom and my brothers in 2011. My new friends and I were at the dining facility eating breakfast on Christmas Eve morning. Just like most of the places on base, in the chow hall there was a big Christmas tree all lit up with fake presents underneath it, and the ornaments were handmade from grade-school kids in the states wishing the troops a merry Christmas.

As we were eating I caught myself just staring at the tree, and I remember it happened like it was with the snap of a finger—

Suddenly I was back sitting on the couch in our old house on Christmas Eve of 2007. I could smell the chicken noodle soup Mom made, still sitting in front of me on the end table untouched because of the giant pit in my stomach. I could see our fake tree by the backdoor all lit up and decorated with our family ornaments. I could see the present I was opening on the ground in front of me, a white Nike sweatshirt with a black football on it. A black fuzzy blanket was draped over me, and a bottle of Acqua Di Gio cologne had been opened, the smell mixing with the chicken noodle soup, creating a sour smell. I could see the headlights shine through the front window behind me, the pit in my stomach roiling and a rush of adrenaline hitting my heart. I could hear the pounding on the door and the anger in my dad's voice and the chair shattering the window above the couch I was sitting on—

"Dude?" my buddies said to me, and I snapped my attention away from the Christmas tree and out of my incredibly vivid vision. I could feel my heart rate pounding through my t-shirt.

"You good?" one of them asked. All of them looked at me like I had a third eye coming out of my head.

"Yeah man, sorry. I just daydream a lot," I said. I felt weird as hell, and a little embarrassed in front of my new friends. Even after snapping back to reality I could feel this rush of energy to my chest, like I just needed to get the hell out of that place as soon as possible. I didn't know it at the time, but I was having a panic attack.

"I'm going to try and Skype my family, guys. I'll talk to you later." I got up from the table and left. On the way home to my dorm room, I saw a police car with its lights on, and suddenly I flashed again. I was in the back of the cop car with Beau, watching them load my mom in the ambulance. I shook it off and focused on the road. When I got to my dorm room, I looked to see if I still had the bottle of cologne I got in 2007, and I did. The flashes started again. I sat in my room and replayed the entire sequence of events from Christmas Eve 2007 over and over and over again. I felt the guilt, the anger, the fear... I felt it all like it was all happening again. Over and over. Again and again.

The beer in my fridge helped drown it out a little bit, but not all. The next thing I knew, it was 3 a.m. Christmas morning. The whole day was a blur, and I hadn't left my dorm since the previous morning. I just ate the cereal I had in my room and finished all the beer that was in my fridge.

I couldn't explain what the hell was happening. The best I surmised was that I was feeling bad for myself.

I just need to man up and get past it, I thought.

The previous week, when I was training at the clinic, I'd met a pararescueman—a PJ, for short—who was in to see the doctor about PTSD. The PJ had probably seen heads blown off. Hell, he probably shot and blew heads off while saving someone else who'd had their leg blown off, and I'm going to sit and fret over my experiences?

"Stop being a pussy. So many people have it worse," I repeatedly told myself.

I never ever considered what was happening to be a symptom of post-traumatic stress disorder, but that's exactly what it was.

The vivid images and even smells...I was there. It was absurdly real, and I couldn't explain or say that to anyone else around me or I would sound crazy. The rising heart rate and rush to my chest and heavy breaths, my fight-or-flight response kicking in.

It was the definition of a panic attack, and over the next several years, it would happen around every Christmas. Sometimes the littlest thing would trigger a response.

I hated Christmas because of what I would turn into. No matter how hard I tried, I would always transport myself back to that night and replay the events over and over.

The only time I didn't have those panic attacks was when I was with my brothers and my mom. I knew they were the only ones who could understand, because they had been there with me and knew the exact same feelings.

SUMMER 2002

"You guys, we can make this happen by the end of the summer, I'm sure of it. All we need is about one hundred more full bags of cans," I said.

The year was 2002, and Devin, Dylan, Chase, and I were counting our bags of cans that we had collected to raise money for our "dream room."

The "dream room" was a term we used for the ultimate fort we were going to build, filled with our favorite things. A giant TV to play video games on, guitars, a drum set, sports memorabilia, bubble hockey, a mini fridge, and a little studio for editing all the movies we were going to make. Most importantly, it would be a place of our own to hang out away from our parents. We had big dreams with our movie ideas and businesses. One day we were going to make millions and reach millions of people doing it. We just knew it. And it wasn't even really about the money— the money was a means to allow us to do what we wanted to do.

With all of our ideas and dreams, we had to be efficient with our time, because Chase and Dylan split time with their divorced parents. Their dad lived about a mile from us and their mom was more than a half hour away.

We knew Chase and Dylan for as long as we could remember, because our dads were friends growing up in the seventies and eighties. In 2001, our family moved out of the trailer park and across town near their dad's, and once we found out how fast we could get to each other's houses on our bikes, we were at theirs when they were with their dad or they were at ours almost every day for the next two to three years. We were always planning our next business venture or writing our next movie plot. There was always a dream being chased. Always.

The four of us made a good team, and we all contributed in different ways. As the oldest, I was the designated leader, and I tried to push our ideas to become reality. Constantly trying to motivate everyone and make things happen in real life, not just keep them ideas like most people do. Most people have a big plan, but they're addicted to the idea that lets them escape. They never actually make it a reality. Whether it was collecting cans to raise money or building a raft to go fishing on, I made sure we all had our vision in focus, tried to keep the crew motivated, and devised plans for us to make the dreams happen. I also was the group worry wart, always thinking of the worst-case scenario and planning ahead to try and avoid any problems...specifically trying to avoid getting in trouble with our dad.

Then you had Dylan and Chase. Dylan was Devin's age and was as motivated as anyone, so when we all decided on our next project and we had our goal, Dylan was all in and nothing was stopping him. He is like that to this day. Chase was four years younger than me, and even at eight years old, he brought creativity in our movies, he could play instruments, which was vital for our future band, Vanilla Twist, and he had the same dreamer mentality as us. Plus, he had a touch of Devin's fearlessness.

Devin rounded out our group as the perfect counterbalance to my worry wartiness. Out of everyone, Devin was the most fearless. If we needed someone to do something dangerous, Deev didn't bat an eye. He'd grab the skateboard and hit the ramp, jump off the roof into the snowbank, or flash his middle finger at authority if he had to.

On the official record of our home movies, there are a number of documented Devin injuries. During our skateboarding phase, Deev hit a ramp we made and "credit carded" the board when he came down. Credit carding means the board hits you between the legs...and it hits him square in the family jewels. In another video, we tried to make our own *Jackass* type movie. We were obsessed with the CKY movies and Bam Margera's crew. Not so much with what they did and said but with the idea of how they lived their lives doing what they wanted to do together as friends. They skateboarded, made movies and skits, and hung out as buddies having fun, always doing what they wanted. That type of freedom was a dream to us, and that's what we wanted. To control our own destinies.

The movie we made wasn't anything like the real *Jackass* movie, but the opening scene is of Devin going down the stairs in a laundry basket and blasting through the sheetrock at the bottom of the stairs. Hilariously, we set a backpack in front of the hole in the wall and nobody noticed until Chase and Dylan's dad sold the house three years later. So, in some sense, we had some unsupervised freedom already.

In one of the last skits of the movie, I was throwing a football up to Devin and when he jumped to catch it, our friend Karl was supposed to hit him midair and tackle him. On the third try, the video shows Devin's legs getting taken out from under him and he gets flipped onto his head, where you can hear a loud *SNAP*. We thought for sure he'd broken his neck, and for the final three days of filming our haggard movie, Devin is laying in the same position on Chase and Dylan's couch. He probably should have gone to the hospital, but we didn't want to get in trouble, so we let him lay there while we finished the film.

In our dream world, the four of us were going to make enough money to build a giant empire and enjoy the things we loved to do. Ideally, our business would revolve around making movies. We were obsessed.

This was the dream room. It was our escape.

That summer, in 2002, we were more motivated than ever to make our dreams a reality. We had built quite a few forts before, including a four-story tree fort in the woods behind our house. We scrounged every two by four and wood pallet we could from around the neighborhood to create a death trap of a fort. On the fourth floor, probably about thirty to forty feet high, you could feel the swaying of the birch trees in the wind and hear the nails creaking as they struggled to claw onto the tree. Looking back, it was pretty incredible what we built, but also very unsafe.

We knew we needed to step up our game and build something professionally, something that could handle all our big dreams. We didn't dare ask our parents for money to build our dream room, because we already knew what the answer would be. Our mom and dad would say, "Figure it out. If you want it bad enough you'll work for it," and Chase and Dylan's dad, Doug, would say something similar: "Welp, go get cans. Back in north-east Brainerd when we were eating ketchup sandwiches we had to go collect cans just to eat. You'll figure it out." Northeast Brainerd was the poor part of town where our dads both grew up, close to where our old trailer park was. They were always telling us how bad they had it and that we had to appreciate everything we had. Part of the reason we worked hard for the things we wanted to do was because we knew for sure that our parents weren't going to just give it to us, so we never asked and tried to figure it out ourselves.

I had some money saved up already from a paper route I did back at the trailer park. At twelve years old, besides a trailer park paper route that paid less than a hundred dollars a month, there wasn't much else for employment. So we took Doug's advice and we collected cans, attending all the adults' football parties solely for the cans. With all the beer they consumed, we were cashing in at least ten to twenty dollars in cans each party. Every once in a while we could be found stealing full beer and pop cans and dumping them out for the few pennies of aluminum, which is hilarious looking back on it. If we were smarter, we would have left the cans full and sold them to the highest high school bidder in our neighborhood...we weren't bad enough kids to think of that at the time.

We had our mind set on the dream room and nothing was going to stop us.

One evening, we were all at our house and we were count-ing our money from can collecting. A few hundred dollars. Not nearly enough yet. We needed at least $500–$600 for the giant TV alone, and we also needed money for lumber to finish off the structure. We'd started building the fort in the woods behind our house, and it was off to a great start. We'd dug a hole about four feet deep and put up four walls and a floor on top of the hole, so we had a mini basement for storage. We even cemented the walls of the basement so the dirt wouldn't cave in on it. The size of the fort wasn't big enough for everything we wanted, but it was a start, and we could add onto it later, I figured, but we needed some more lumber and a roof, so we definitely needed a lot more money. We also had thousands of arcade tickets, which we figured we could use to buy a bunch of the sports memorabilia we wanted.

I had all the faith in the world that we would succeed. I *knew* we would succeed and we would live out our dreams.

All we have to do is put in the work and keep being a team, I thought.

That evening, after we counted our first few hundred dollars of can collecting, I got a jar and planned on keeping it in my closet, right next to Grandpa's gray metal box. I planned on keeping it there until we'd saved enough money to make our first big purchase. After we labeled and stuffed the jar that night, I went to put it in my closet, and through the floor vents, I could hear my parents arguing in the basement, where their room was at the time. My mentality shifted from motivated dreamer mode to defensive mode, thinking about all the worst-case scenarios with my dad and planning on how I was going to tiptoe around and stay out of his way. If they were arguing, it probably meant that it would spill over into the next day.

brrrrEEEEP. From down the hall I heard Devin with Dylan and two of their other friends make a loud fart noise in Devin's room. Generally, this is the type of thing that would have had me dying of laughter, but not now, when I knew Dad and Mom were arguing. I tiptoed to Devin's room and warned them, "Guys, I'd be quiet. He's pissed off tonight, I can hear them arguing. Just be quiet." Dylan and Chase knew enough to know my dad had a tendency to snap, and when he did, you didn't want to be around.

brrrrEEEEP. Another giant fart followed by laughter. Devin's two other friends had no idea, and I shouldn't have expected them to understand, but I thought everyone's dad was like mine.

I walked back to my room and laid on my bed. It was getting late, about 11 p.m., and I just knew that the later it went and the louder the arguing got, the worse the reaction was going to be.

The laughter and noise from Deev's room was louder and louder.

Dad was going to be mad. I could feel it. A bunch of eleven-year-olds laughing at farts and being stupid. How dare they.

Sure enough…*THUMP. THUMP. THUMP.*

His footsteps up the stairs to Devin's room shook the house.

He got to Devin's room, and the boys in the room went silent.

"Turn on the fuckin' light," Dad slurred.

There was nothing.

"NOWWWWW!" he screamed at the top of his lungs.

"You think that's funny, huh?" I could only hear what was going on, but later found out from Devin that Dad had grabbed Devin by the shirt collar and dragged him out of his bedroom and down the stairs to the basement where Mom was.

"Put him down, now!" Mom pleaded. "I'm calling the cops right now!"

There was silence for about a minute. I ran over to the metal box in my closet and grabbed my hunting knife. I laid back down in my bed, and I clenched my eyes shut, praying to God to make him stop whatever was happening. I held onto my knife.

*Thump thump thump...*I heard Devin's footsteps scurrying back to his room. I heard him shut the door and just heard the "s" noises of the whispers from him and his friends, but that's about it. I heard nothing else from downstairs, and after about an hour, I let myself shut my eyes and go to sleep.

In the morning, Dad left for work and my brother's friends left.

"Dude, what the heck happened last night downstairs?" I asked Devin.

He went on to explain that after he was dragged downstairs, Dad had grabbed a small toy we had, which was a handheld drum, a monkey drum-like toy, and he raised it up above Devin's head like he was going to bash him with it in front Mom, which is when I heard Mom threaten to call the cops. Devin said he just tucked his head and waited for the blows when all of a sudden he let Devin go, and that's when Devin ran back upstairs to his bedroom.

After Devin told me the story, I felt relieved that Dad wasn't home for the day, but we had to face him that evening, and I dreaded it. Was he still going to be pissed off? Was he actually going to hit Devin or someone else next time? It was too far into the future, I convinced myself, and we had work to do. Dylan and Chase had to be back at their mom's that evening, and we had more cans to collect before they did.

We have to make the dream room happen ASAP, I thought.

If we had our own fort to hang out in, we wouldn't have even been in that situation the night before. They could be as loud as they wanted and make all the fart noises they wanted in the dream room.

We didn't know it at the time, but we already had the dream room we so longed for. We escaped to the dream room every day when we chased our dreams with Dylan and Chase. We blocked everything out when we dreamed, and as big as our dreams and ambitions were, nobody could touch us when we were high on them. Not even our dad.

I wasn't expecting to go home until my two years in Japan were done. Every penny I made, I saved. That was my whole reason for joining the Air Force in the first place—money problems—and I wasn't going to waste any of it on dumb things. To me, my time in the Air Force was a means to an end, and I didn't care about anything else but getting done with my four years so I could resume my life. I didn't see it at the time, but this view about my time in the military was just how I justified withdrawing from the world and socially isolating, another sign of PTSD. That's how I coped with everything after my Christmas that year. The last thing I wanted to feel was that embarrassment in front of my friends again, so I just avoided any and all of those situations as often as I could so it couldn't happen.

Luckily, I wouldn't have to spend any money to go home. I was assigned to a flight medicine clinic. Flight medicine was responsible for taking care of anyone who flew in a plane, from pilots to the flight crew. Anyone who flew for their Air Force duties required extra medical attention on their physicals. The clinic was also responsible for any flight mishap investigations. If an aircraft crashes, an investigation needs to be conducted to see exactly why it crashed, and flight medicine is a very large part of conducting that investigation. The part that was lucky for me was that working in flight medicine required extra training, specifically on the crash investigation process. The training was in Ohio, and after just two months at my new duty station, I would be flying back to the states on the government's dime. Then when I was done, I would be able to take some more leave and visit home again, and that's exactly what I did.

After I got done with my training, I flew home and took a week of leave. I was excited to hang out with my friends again, and Devin was supposed to be home. It would be the first time I saw him in at least a year. A few months before I joined the Air Force, Devin moved to Colorado to work, so I was excited to catch up with him and see how he was doing. I hadn't told anyone about my Christmastime flashbacks or panic attacks, but I was hoping to hear if maybe Deev was experiencing the same things. I was scared to tell anyone about it, but if anyone would understand it, it would be my brother.

When I arrived home, I realized I wouldn't be doing much talking with Devin about anything. When I walked into my mom's, Devin was there with his new girlfriend, Emma. My excitement to see him and meet her faded when I dropped my bags and walked into the kitchen. Before she reached out to shake my hand I could tell that she was obliterated, and it was obvious that it wasn't just alcohol. I guessed she was high on some sort of pills, because I'd seen this too many times before. I didn't know exactly what else they were high on, but it wasn't my normal brother Devin who I was talking to. My sixth sense that I'd spent seventeen years developing knew something wasn't right.

We were at Mom's together for about five minutes before one of Devin's friends picked them up, and they left to go to a party. I was home for a week before I flew back to Japan. I didn't see Devin or his girlfriend again that entire time and wouldn't see Deev again for almost two years.

CHAPTER 7

It had been a week since the incident. Mom was out of the hospital after a few surgeries on her face, and Christmas break was over. My brothers, Mom, and I were still staying with our aunt and uncle at their trailer house south of town. It was nice being there, because they didn't have neighbors. Quiet, calm, and isolated. The last thing my brothers and I wanted to do was go back to school. I had talked to my best friends once I got my phone back a few days before, and I'd told them a little bit about what had happened, but as far as I knew, nobody else could have known about it unless my friends told them. So I convinced myself that it couldn't be that bad at school since only a few people knew about it...

Until I saw the newspaper that morning.

"Baxter Man Accused of Attempted Murder," read the headline of the *Brainerd Daily Dispatch*.

My heart sank... Now every kid in my class of 500 students and high school of 2,000+ students would know. Aside from the newspaper article, I didn't realize it at the time, because I didn't even know it existed, but a favorite pastime of people who live in smaller towns is checking the "in custody report" of the county jails online, especially on Monday mornings or mornings after a holiday and long weekend. Everyone knew.

"You don't have to go," Mom said, "But I think showing up to school shows strength, and it shows that no matter what he does, he can't hurt you anymore. I think it's a good example to set."

Mom is right, I thought. *I need to be an example for my brothers.* If I stayed home, they would probably do the same. Still, the idea of going to school sucked.

"Screw it. Man the hell up, Dez," I said to myself, trying to build some sort of layer of defense in my head before I went to school. Hell, I drove around with whiskey plates for an entire year and my own football teammates talked about that in front of my face. Who knows what everyone said behind my back? That gossip didn't faze me then, so why should it faze me now? I just had to block it out and not care what people thought.

Easy. Everyone must have known something wasn't right already. Besides, who truly cares what people think? Everyone talks and they always will. I'll be out of school in a year and a half, and all of these people will be behind me.

That's where I stopped with building my defense, looking forward to the end of high school in a year and a half.

"Just a year and a half," I said.

I didn't care about any of the good things like being a football and baseball captain my senior year, didn't care about prom, didn't care about grades...just the end of it. Once I was gone, I didn't have to worry about what people said anymore.

To further mentally prepare myself, I decided to get to school early that first morning back and lift weights. I figured that maybe doing something physical would wear me out a bit, and the exhaustion would deter any worry that might arise when I saw my friends.

When I got to the weight room, there was a senior lifting along with one of the football coaches. That was surprising. It took an extra motivated high schooler to get their ass in the gym at 6 a.m. before school, and I wasn't even there because I was motivated. They both asked, "How was your break? Did you guys stay in town or travel?" The usual small talk. They had no idea what had happened.

Perfect, I thought.

I walked to the weight rack tucked away in the back corner, hidden from anyone who might walk in. I started stretching, loaded some weights onto the bench, sat down, and did a set. I sat up and put my elbows on my knees.

I had been talking to God a lot the previous few days. I'd thanked him many times for keeping my brothers and Mom alive, prayed for him to give us strength going forward, especially strength on the first day back, and as I sat there between sets, I found myself asking him: *Why? Why did this have to happen?*

DECEMBER 24TH, 2007

After I put the hunting knife in my pocket, I closed Grandpa's box and put it back under my bed. I packed a few pairs of clothes for the weekend at my dad's and walked upstairs where my mom and brothers were already waiting to go.

"Mom, where are you going while we are at Dad's?" I asked.

"I'm heading over to Jess and Luke's, then I'll be back home later," she said.

"What if we don't want to stay at Dad's?" I said.

"Things will be fine, Desmond."

"He's been texting me weird stuff all afternoon. Something isn't right."

"You guys need to get over there. We're already over an hour late."

I shook my head. The last place I wanted to be at that moment was Dad's. The texts had stopped an hour ago, so I was hoping that maybe he'd calmed down before we arrived.

We got into my car, and I drove down the road to Dad's apartment. "He's being weird, man. I think he's drinking," I said to Devin on our way. We parked, grabbed our bags and the few gifts for our dad, and walked through the snowy parking lot.

Dad's apartment was on the first floor, and we used the sliding door to come and go. As soon as I slid the door open and walked inside, my body tightened. I hadn't even seen him yet, and I knew for certain he was drinking again. I didn't see any bottles, but I knew the signs well enough to know. Rock music was blaring, and there was smoke in the kitchen and two trays full of tater tots sitting on the stove top. One thing my dad did when he got too messed up was cook an abnormal amount of junk food, and it often got burnt because he would be standing in the kitchen on the verge of passing out while he was supposed to be taking whatever he was cooking out of the oven. It ended the same every time.

One time, he almost burnt the house down when he put a bag of popcorn in the microwave for way too long. Walking upstairs the following morning, the stench hit me right away. Then, as I walked into my mom and dad's room, Mom said, "You know what your dad did last night? He almost burnt the house down." They had clearly been arguing about the burnt bag of popcorn, and how frequently it happened. Dad had started laughing like it wasn't a big deal and genuinely funny. I didn't think it was funny then, and I didn't think it was funny that night at his apartment.

"There you guys are! Your mom leave already?!" He popped around the corner as we walked in. Slurring like a stroke victim. Sarcasm with spite in his tone.

"No, Dad, I drove my car over. It's just us," I said.

"Oh, too bad. I made lots of food!" He walked into the smoky kitchen and took a tray of burnt pizza rolls from the oven, setting the tray next to the burnt tater tots.

I walked in and assessed the situation further, my senses working at 100 percent and trying to figure out what I was going to do with my brothers if we had to get out of there. I was looking for any other sign of him drinking, specifically any bottles of booze. I already knew he was drunk, but I needed the hard proof to validate my suspicions. My brothers were in the living room putting the presents under the tree. Dad was playing air guitar in the kitchen to the rock music.

"Beau, you have this one on your little game? That game you're so focused on when you come over here and just play the whole time?" my dad said. More spite in his tone, this time directed at Beau, which was something that was unusual and caused me even more alarm. I didn't ever remember him directing his ire at Beau. I tried my best to act like we didn't know he was being weird.

"Have you seen him though, Dad?" I said pointing at Beau. "I think he could actually win tournaments. Beau mops the floor with all of us at that game!" The game we were talking about was Guitar Hero, and it was genuinely bizarre how good Beau was at it, even at eleven years old.

Dad ignored me and continued his air guitar.

He is being extra weird, I thought.

He had to know we knew he was drinking again, right after getting out of rehab. It's like he didn't even care one bit that we might have known, which was another reason for me to be on alert. After all the crying a few months before and saying he was going to change, it's like he was saying screw it and screw all of you too.

"I have to piss," I said and walked to the bathroom and locked the door.

I took out my phone and texted my mom. *Mom, he's messed up. We're not staying here. He's being really weird.*

I looked around the bathroom and there they were. The empty bottles of beer in the trash can along with empty prescription pill bottles. I didn't bother to look at what the prescriptions were, and I had no clue if he had taken any of them with his beer. All I knew was that there were several empty pill bottles in the trash can with the empty beer bottles.

I shook my head. I'd already known it, but seeing the empty bottles there killed me. Dad told me he was going to rehab for my brothers and me, to be a good dad, and he'd lied. The hard proof was right before me. Before he'd left for Hazelden, he'd hugged me on the top step of our house. He'd told me he loved me, and for whatever reason, he'd also said, "You're better than this town, Desmond. When you can, leave it. You have a big future ahead of you." I'd hugged my dad and cried with him. I wanted him to get better, and I was relieved that he wanted to too. I was sad to see my dad in so much pain, even if I had bad memories of him when he was drunk, but I was proud as hell of him for wanting to change. He was my only dad, and I loved him.

Now standing in his bathroom, all of that seemed like a lie.

We're leaving as soon as we get a chance. Something doesn't feel safe, I texted my mom again.

Okay, call me as soon as you leave, Mom texted back almost immediately. She knew I was making the right call.

I knew we couldn't just get up and go or he'd flip out. We would have to sneak out.

I got to the living room where my brothers were sitting, our dad still in the kitchen. I sat down and made eye contact with Devin. When Dad left the kitchen to go to the back room, presumably to have another beer, I whispered, "We're leaving. He's messed up and this is not okay, and I don't know about you guys, but something feels off. We're going to sneak out so keep your coats and shoes by you." Both Devin and Beau nodded. I could see it in their faces that they were just as uncomfortable as I was.

Dad came back to the room. "You know what you guys should do? You should take candy canes and put them on the doors of the other apartments in the hall. There's lots of little kids who would love it," he slurred.

This could be our chance to sneak out, I thought. *We'll go put the candy canes on the doors and then we'll walk out the front door of the building.*

I felt a buzz in my pocket and I looked at my phone. *Leave yet?* Mom's text read.

As soon as I read the text, my dad left the room again and closed his door.

This is it.

I nodded to my brothers toward the sliding door, and we all got up and left the apartment. We didn't run, but we walked fast to the car, got in, then sped off down the road.

I called my mom. "Mom, he's messed up. There were empty beer bottles and pill bottles in the bathroom. Something is wrong with him. He seems pretty pissed too," I said.

"Okay, I'll see you back at the house—" she began.

"Mom, no. We can't go back to the house. I'm telling you, he's going to do something. I know it. We can't go home."

"Where are you guys?"

"I'm pulling into the Best Buy parking lot right now. Come meet us here," I said. The Best Buy was half a mile from Dad's apartment, and we sat there for two minutes before Mom pulled up next to us.

My phone vibrated. Dad was calling. I let it go to voicemail.

I opened it and let the message play on speaker so Mom could hear from the other car with our windows rolled down. "Where did you go, Desmond? One minute you're here, and then POOF, you and your brothers are gone!" His slurring was even worse.

"We can't go home, Mom," I said again.

"Well, what are we supposed to do? It's Christmas Eve," Mom said.

"I don't know. Let's drive back to Thief River Falls, go to Dan and LaCoe's, get a hotel. We just can't go home." Dan and LaCoe were our friends down the street. They were like family, and they knew better than anyone the issues my family had. They had seen it firsthand for years. Dan helped coach our baseball teams and was one of my dad's best friends. They were some of the best people I knew, and I knew they would understand if we went to their house, even if it was Christmas Eve. I just knew we couldn't go home that night. Anywhere but home. None of us were going to stop him if he tried to do anything. He was a huge guy.

"We can't go to Dan and LaCoe's. They have their own Christmas stuff going on with the boys. He's not going to do anything if we go home."

"Mom, yes he is. I'm telling you. I've been talking to him all day and something in him snapped. It's like he doesn't even care anymore."

"Desmond, we have to go home," she said, "Come on, we'll figure it out when we get home." She started driving away, and I followed her.

This is not a good idea, I thought.

We parked and went inside. The first thing I did was take my shoes off at the front door and carry them downstairs to my bedroom. A few years before, Devin and I both moved our rooms downstairs. My bedroom had a large egress window in it, and I pulled the screen off of it and set the screen behind my dresser. I set my shoes right under the window and made sure the window was unlocked by cranking it all the way open before shutting it again.

We need another way to escape if we have to, I thought.

If he was as drunk as I suspected he was, all we had to do was get out of the house, and he wasn't chasing us very far in his condition. I had to prepare us all for the worst-case scenario. Mom hadn't seen the severity of it, and if I was wrong, then good. I hoped I was. But I knew I wasn't.

I walked upstairs to where my brothers were sitting in the living room. Beau was sorting a few gifts my mom had for us that were supposed to be opened in a few days when we got back from our dad's. I had completely forgotten it was Christmas Eve. It was the last thing on my mind, and I couldn't have cared less about opening a present that night.

Mom was in the kitchen heating up some chicken noodle soup. When she brought it to us, the pit in my stomach was so hard that I could barely even sniff the soup without gagging. I was not hungry in the least. I wouldn't have been able to take a sip of water if I wanted to.

My phone vibrated. Dad again. I let it ring... No voicemail this time.

"You guys can open your presents," Mom said.

We opened our gifts. I opened up a box that contained a white sweatshirt with a black Nike football on it and a bottle of Acqua Di Gio cologne. I sprayed it on my hand to smell it, and I thought it smelled great...just not with the chicken noodle soup aroma mixing with it. I set the shirt and cologne back in the box and wrapped myself up with a black fuzzy blanket, which was a gift from our mom a few Christmases before. I went to grab the second gift to open when from the window behind where I was sitting, I saw headlights glare into the living room. They got brighter and brighter as they came closer and parked right outside of the window. I heard the door *slam*, the footsteps up the wooden stairs to our front door *DUMPF, DUMPF, DUMPF* and the *POUND, POUND, POUND* of his fist before I heard, "OPEN THE FUCKIN' DOOR! NOOOOOOOOOW!"

CRASHHHHHHH the sound of glass from the window above me shattering...

I sat on the workout bench reliving the scene for the thousandth time in the week since it had happened. I looked up at the clock and realized I had been sitting there for at least fifteen minutes. Luckily nobody else in the room noticed. At least it didn't seem like it. Sitting there for fifteen minutes and not lifting a single weight, just reliving my Christmas break—it wasn't like I was trying to relive it or sit and feel sorry for myself and my family. I just found myself dissecting the whole thing, in partial denial that it had even happened, because it all felt so surreal still, and I was trying to figure out how I could have stopped it all. The other part that I couldn't figure out was why? When I sat and thought of this stuff, the event would start replaying, and once it started, it was hard to stop. Like a movie, it just kept going. I questioned whether or not I should be there at school that day after all. Maybe I should just leave...

From the other end of the weight room, I saw one of my football coaches, Coach Hock. There wasn't one coach I had that I didn't respect and consider someone I trusted, but coach Hock was my favorite. He wasn't a hardass by any means, but he knew how to let me know I wasn't playing to my potential. I had him as a coach when I was a sophomore, and one of the first two-a-day practices that fall we were doing our end of practice conditioning. That day, we ran "Warrior 200s," which were simply running from goal line to goal line, usually about five times. On the first run down and back, I finished near the front with the fastest seniors and juniors, definitely top fifteen finishers of well over one hundred players.

Hock walked up to me in front of the whole team and yelled, "What are you doing, Janousek!? You are one of the fastest guys out of anyone here. You should be in the front every single time. If you are cheating yourself, you are cheating your teammates! You're a leader here, act like it!"

He's right, I thought. *I can't take it easy. I need to be an example.*

On the next three 200s, I finished in first by ten yards each time. I felt like my heart was about to explode, but by pushing myself that day I knew how much more I could give and what was possible. It was just as much a mental game as it was a physical one. I had to put out more. I had to do the right thing and do my best. For myself and for the team.

This translated onto the field. I was the quarterback and cornerback on defense of the sophomore team that year, and we didn't lose a game, 8-0. One game we were losing in the middle of a blizzard against Alexandria. Hock pulled me aside and said, "We need you here. You can do this." On that drive, I ran in an eighty-yard TD, and we won by seven.

Coach Hock had the ability to bring out the best in me, and for that I loved playing for him. I think it's easy to dismiss our teenage sporting experiences, but at least on the team I was a part of, I learned a lot of things that are applicable to my everyday life. And for that, I am eternally grateful.

I was still sitting at my workout bench in the back, and Coach Hock saw me sitting there. He started walking back toward me. I wondered if he had seen the newspaper or if he'd just ask me how my Christmas break was like my other coach and teammate.

I stood up to shake his hand, and instead, he reached out his arms and hugged me.

"I can't tell you how happy I am to see you here today," he said.

All my worry about school that day faded. I was supposed to be there. I needed to be there.

CHAPTER 8

MARCH 2012

After my short stint back home for Flight Medicine training, I flew back to Japan. I did so without getting to see Devin before I left. I only knew he and his new girlfriend went back to Colorado because Mom told me. I'd have my weekly phone call with her on my Saturday mornings, which would have been her Friday evenings. I started getting used to being up early in the mornings, because the Vikings played at 3 a.m. on Monday mornings in Japan. That was part of easing into my early morning routine, and I was also the PT monitor of my flight, so I *had* to work out at 5 a.m. with all of the people who were in danger of failing their PT tests. I hated it. I would show up at 5 a.m. to help motivate the out-of-shape flight members so they didn't get kicked out of the Air Force, only to find them eating a double whopper and drinking supersized Coke for lunch that same day. Maddening, to say the least.

For anyone who has no experience with the military, this is a common thing. A very large percentage of the military is filled with obese and unhealthy people, and it's in every branch.

Some eventually get kicked out, but others know how to do just enough to get by. That, and physical standards continue to ease. It's a shame. I didn't understand how these people could let themselves go and not have at least some respect for themselves.

You're in the military! I thought.

But I didn't understand at the time that you can't help someone with their weight and fitness if they don't want to be helped. It's the same with any addiction, whether it be to food, alcohol, drugs... The only person who can make an addict change is the addict themselves.

My routine in Japan became a well-oiled machine. I'd get up, work out, go to the dining facility for breakfast, go to work at the flight medicine clinic, get off at 4 p.m., grab dinner to go from the dining facility, put my dinner in the fridge in my dorm room, and then I would go run the Habu Trail on base. The Habu Trail was a one-and-a-half-mile stretch of isolated path that was tucked away in a corner of the base, on a little offshoot away from the flightline and the main hangouts. When I ran it, I felt like I was running in a jungle. I'd run down and back for three miles and I would time myself, always trying to shave a few seconds and see how fast I could go.

Afterward, I would go back to my dorm and shower, I'd eat dinner, then I would spend an hour writing and an hour reading. My goal each day was to write 500 words and read at least fifty pages of whatever I was reading, mostly financial books and books about film. I wrote because I knew the importance of being a good writer. With good writing and communication, you can do anything. You can create great books and movies that inspire you or you can become the CEO of a company, or even the president (for better or for worse). More importantly, I knew it was like working out—you *have* to write often to get better at it.

So I read and wrote every day. During my two years in Japan, I wrote two movie scripts, a novel, and at least forty short stories. Most importantly, I did all of this because I never let go of the dream, the one that Chase, Dylan, Devin, and I had imagined ten years before. I wanted to create things and help people in one way or another with the creations. Most were humorous stories, because I truly thought that helped people. At the time, there was no such thing as a "content creator" or "social media influencer." YouTube was in its infant stages still and other social media sites didn't even exist. Back then, my goal was to find a film school and hopefully some like-minded people to help me turn my ideas into a reality. I hated the idea of college but saw the value in the community where I might be able to find people in a similar headspace of wanting to create things. In order to do that, I needed to get better at writing, and I needed to study, and that's what I did while I was in Japan.

Each evening, after I was done reading and writing, I would watch something before bed, usually comedic. This, to me, was also a form of studying. I became obsessed with Bill Hicks, Sam Kinison, and Bill Burr, how they were able to make people laugh while also talking about very serious issues. They were brilliant.

Afterward, I would go to bed. Then I would wake up and do it all again the next day.

All of this time I spent mostly by myself. I justified it by thinking I was bettering myself for the future, and I was—I was preparing myself for success, which included undertaking all of the hard work I was doing there every day. I didn't realize what I was really doing, beneath the surface, was that I had almost completely socially withdrawn. Aside from work, I rarely went out or saw friends. I had a few good friends who would invite me on weekends, but after a while they stopped. After the incident in the chow hall that Christmas, I felt humiliated, and my way to prevent it from happening again was to withdraw. In my head, I saw my time in Japan as my time to improve myself physically and mentally—improve my writing skills and study film and finance as much as I could so I could get out and make everything happen as I envisioned it. This was during my first six months in Japan, until I met Master Sergeant Denson.

When I first got to Japan, Denson was deployed to Afghanistan, but I would hear stories about him from my flight.

"He's crazy, man," I would hear. "I saw him tell a full-bird colonel to go to hell. Right in front of the general. He's insane."

When he got back from Afghanistan, I found out what all of my coworkers were talking about. He was, in fact, crazy.

One morning, our flight surgeon had a full schedule of patients, and Denson, on his first day of duties after his deployment, was making his rounds to our flight members exchanging hellos. Before he got to me to introduce himself, he looked at the flight surgeon's schedule at the front desk, and I could hear him say, "No. no. no. That son of a bitch still thinks I'm deployed, I bet."

He walked over to me. "You're the new airman here, Janousek? Come with me. I'm about to teach you something."

I walked with Denson back to a patient room where a patient was already waiting for the flight surgeon. The patient was Captain Johnson, a pilot who flew C-17s. Captain Johnson was in to see the flight surgeon for a "profile." The captain was a bit overweight, and in my short experience at the flight, I figured he was in to get a profile so he could skip his PT test or he'd fail and get in trouble. I saw people like this almost daily at the clinic. It was unfortunate, because some people had real injuries and needed a profile, but the system was abused by people like Captain Johnson, and Master Sergeant Denson apparently already knew this about him.

Denson opened the door, and I followed him inside. The captain sat up a little straighter, recognizing Denson when we walked in. The door shut behind us.

"A PT profile?" Denson asked the captain.

"Yep, I have an injured—"

"You have a weight problem, son," Denson said, cutting off the captain. "You're not injured. You want a profile to skip your PT test."

There was silence between the three of us, as Denson and the captain engaged in a stare-off.

At first I was a little taken back. An enlisted member speaking to an officer like that?

WOW, I thought.

"This is what we're going to do," Denson said. "You're going to get a profile today, but then you're going to take your fat ass to the gym and start eating right. You're a damn captain in the Air Force, a pilot no less. Get your shit together, son."

And that was it. We left the room, and Denson didn't say anything to me about the incident the rest of the day. Was he using the opportunity to posture with me and show me how crazy he was and not to cross him? Was he trying to help me? Was he trying to help Captain Johnson?

Over the next few weeks, I started to get to know Denson, because I shared an office with him and three other airmen. He was smarter than anyone in the squadron, including any officer.

He had been promoted to master sergeant as fast as you possibly could in the Air Force, because up until E7, most of the promotion requirements are written tests. It's a joke, for the most part. Merit has little to do with it. On that portion of the promotions, it's who can take the written tests the best and who can play politician the best on their "merit" packages. For example, on "merit and accomplishments," if you picked up trash on the base, you could say something like, "Saved the Air Force twenty million dollars in potential environmental disaster with a runway FOD cleaning program." Technically not lying, but also full of crap. Denson knew this game well and how it worked, and it's exactly how he got promoted to E7 as fast as you possibly can. He was smart but definitely a little crazy.

In the office, after I started to get a better feel for him, I asked him, "Hey remember Captain Johnson? What made you talk to him like that? Didn't you think he'd report you for that?"

Without looking up from what he was doing, he said, "He lost his anchor, and clearly everyone else is too afraid to tell him what the real problem is. Bunch of pussies now in the military across the board. Sometimes what people really need is a kick in the ass, and I tried to give it to him."

"Lost his anchor?" I asked.

"Lost his anchor."

At my desk, I had a book about technical trading and the stock market. I had been obsessed with the stock market since I was a kid. When we were younger, I saw it as a possible way that we could make money and fund our dream room. I had heard stories about people like Warren Buffet and thought, *If he can do it, why can't we?* Unfortunately, our parents would not co-sign a brokerage account for us at twelve years old, so we had to resort to collecting cans until we could get jobs. But that's how I still view the stock market. It was never about getting rich and buying lavish things, but buying freedom and funding the things we really wanted to do. I also thought, and still think, what an amazing opportunity—any person out there can spend ten to twenty dollars and buy a share of a company like Ford and be a part of one of the most important American companies.

He saw my book and asked, "Are you taking classes or what?"

"What classes?" I was genuinely confused.

"Like college classes. You must be, if you're reading that boring garbage."

"No. I just like learning about the markets and how they work. It's a big game of psychology. If you can master it, you don't have to worry about money anymore and can focus on other things."

"Well, if you're willing to read about that boring crap, then I got a book for you. I just finished it." Denson reached into his backpack and pulled out *The Game* by Neil Strauss.

"What's this about?" I asked.

"Psychology." He handed me the book and left the office.

By the end of the work day, I had read the first few chapters, and I was hooked. I went and grabbed dinner and skipped my run so I could get back to my dorm room and read more. The book was about this guy, Neil Strauss, who infiltrated a group of male "pickup artists." These guys would get together and talk about techniques on how to go out to bars and seduce women. It was bizarre but fascinating what these guys would do to try and get women to want them and what would work. Denson was right in that it was a book about psychology.

Before I knew it, it was almost midnight, and I had finished the entire book in one evening.

The next day, I set the book on Denson's desk so I didn't forget to return it to him. When he walked in and saw it, he asked, "What's this?"

"I finished it last night," I said.

"You what?"

"I finished the book. It was amazing. It's one of the best books I have read in a while," I said.

"I just gave this to you. Like yesterday," he said.

"I know. It was just too good to put down. It's literally all I did after work. Thanks for letting me read it."

The following day, Denson told me to come to his car after work because "he had a few more books for me."

When the clinic closed, we walked to his car and from the back seat, he pulled out a big plastic tote and set it on the ground.

"I'm going to tell you this right now, and I'm serious. Neil Gaiman used to say he liked the excitement of reading a new book because he didn't know how it would change him afterward, and it's true. It can screw with your head. So, have an anchor."

"You've said that before. What the hell does it mean?"

"It means, have a damn anchor. Don't go crazy."

That still didn't clarify much for me.

"I've got training in Bali for a few months, and I'll be back. We'll talk about whatever you read then. If you like psychology, then here you go. I got my master's in psychology, and if you want to learn more about it, there's lots in here."

He handed me a book titled *Meditations* by Marcus Aurelius. He loaded the tote of books into my car and left. I wouldn't see him again for two months.

When I got back to my building that afternoon and heaved the tote up the stairs to my dorm room, I sat and sifted through it for the next few hours trying to decide what I wanted to read next. There were at least forty books and a pretty wide variety. There were military strategy books, lots of philosophy and religion, and a few classics like *Crime and Punishment.*

Over the next few months I spent my evenings and weekends devouring books like *The Prince, Crystallizing Public Opinion, 12 Life Lessons* by St Thomas Aquinas, parts of The Quran, and everything by Nietzsche. It was wide ranging in ideology. Things I had never even heard of before.

Ever since I was a kid, the question "why" lingered. Why do people do what they do? Why would my dad act like he did sometimes? Some of these books were dark looks at human behavior and posed questions I had never thought of about morality and God. Some of them gave me a cynical view about things for a while, but some provided answers. As I continued searching, more questions arose. So I read more.

When I was a kid, Mom would bring us to the public library every week. It was one of my favorite things to do. When we arrived, I would go straight to the baseball section and research the greats. I memorized their stats and achievements. When I was there, my mind was not in the library, I was transported to a baseball game watching Mark McGuire and Sammy Sosa chasing 61. My favorite place in the summer time was the baseball field, so in the winter time the library took me there again. I found out on our trips the magic that could happen with a great story. Your mind doesn't think about anything else. You're in another place. When we were about to leave, we got to pick out a few movies for the next week, and with our library cards we got to rent them for free. These library escapes showed me the power of good stories and fueled my desire to make my own. I wanted to be the creator who helped others escape.

Two months went by, and Denson came back from his training deployment. I had read at least two dozen of the books from the tote. I was looking forward to discussing them with him. I'd tried a few times to talk with my friends about some of the things I was reading and thinking about, but they didn't seem to have much interest in exploring the ideas, so to avoid seeming like a pretentious asshole, I'd stopped bringing it up.

When I first saw Denson back in the office, something didn't seem right. I wondered if maybe he had seen some messed up stuff on his training mission. He was still crazier than a shithouse rat flipping the bird at authority but a little extra crazy after his deployment. For example, he would show up to our morning flight workouts and get out of his car at 5 a.m. with a cigar in his mouth already half smoked. Then he would proceed to run the Habu Trail and beat everyone besides me. It was pretty impressive, to be honest, but he was not himself from before his training deployment. Some mornings, he'd show up to work, and I could tell he was hungover or even drunk still, and clearly not showered from his ruffled hair and odor.

Finally one day, I said, "Dude, you've been walking around like your dog died since you got back. What's the deal?"

He sat for a second, then said, "My wife..."

Aw damn it, I thought. *Way to put your foot in your mouth.*

"When I got back from Bali," he continued, "my wife tells me she's Pentecostal now."

I felt a bit of a relief. "Jeez man, you had me there for a second. I thought you were about to say she cheated on you or something." I thought for sure his wife cheated on him. It was something that was as common as the sun rising in the military. I worked with about ten senior enlisted sergeants in my flight, and all but two had been divorced at least once. It's just not a lifestyle conducive to a healthy relationship. The only relationships I saw doing well (at least on the surface) were ones that prioritized church in their lives.

He laughed. "Naw, she's speaking in tongues now, and she hated church before. It's just been messing with me since I got back, that's all. I honestly appreciate you asking. If I'm ever too far off the reservation, let me know. Sometimes it's hard to see it yourself."

"Well, it could always be worse man. I thought something was up, but never would have guessed that was what the deal was."

RING RING RING RING RING!!!

The crash phone at our clinic blared. This was a very important part of being in Flight Medicine and one of the main reasons I'd gone to training in Ohio when I first got to Japan. When the crash phone rang, it was the air traffic control tower calling us for medical assistance, and it meant that there was a medical emergency or potential emergency on the flight line or with an airborne aircraft.

Whenever a pilot radioed in an emergency, air traffic control would call our clinic. They would give us the nature of emergency, type of aircraft, and number of people involved, and then we (whoever was on ambulance duty at the time) would grab our radios, drop whatever we were doing, and would drive the ambulance about a mile away to the flight line to provide medical assistance. Generally it was just two medics who would respond, but on any serious call, we would bring a flight surgeon.

This crash phone rang almost daily, and 99 percent of the time, it was precautionary. Oftentimes I would get the info from air traffic control and the emergency would be "engine out," which was a big nothing burger. The P-3 planes that are older than dirt had four engines, so if one was out, it really didn't matter, but we would still have to drive the ambulance to the flight line, park at the base of the air traffic control tower, and wait for the P-3 to land. We would then wait to get the all clear before we could leave. We were there just in case.

A few of the more serious emergencies we had responded to still weren't too crazy. On one call, there was an F-15 pilot who had cabin depressurization, and when we responded to him landing, we put him in the back of the ambulance and drove him to the dive chamber, where they simulated "diving" him under water so the gasses in his blood didn't get to his brain and give him the benz and potentially kill him. On another call, an F-15 pilot parked his jet and the hood of the jet wouldn't open, so we responded and sat there until the maintenance crew opened it and he got out.

That morning when the phone was ringing, I expected nothing different. I walked over to the office secretary, who was still on the phone with air traffic control writing down information about the emergency. She hung up and handed me the piece of paper. At the top, it said: "NOE (Nature of Emergency): *HH60 crash.*"

"Holy shit," I said. "Denson, we gotta go."

I grabbed the flight surgeon, and the three of us were off to the crash site.

Generally on our calls, we drove down the street to the flight line on the Air Base, but on this call, the crash site was on one of the Marine bases about twenty minutes away, so we had to drive off base. Driving a giant ambulance on the roads of Okinawa is not ideal. The lanes are made for their tiny compact cars.

When we got to the Marine base, I could see black smoke in the distance, at least a mile away, coming from the green jungle hills of the Marine training base. We drove through one of the main gates, past a crowd of Japanese activists already out with signs, at least a few dozen of them. This was not the first time I'd seen activists at the gates of the several different military bases on Okinawa. Over the years, there had been several incidents with aircraft crashing on the island and service members assaulting Japanese women that fueled these protests.

Since 1972, there had been forty-three aircraft crashes on Okinawa, including one in 2004 where a Marine helicopter crashed into one of the universities. Luckily, school was on break at the time. I knew of this incident because during my first week at Kadena Air Base I received an email notifying the entire base about a "gate closure due to protestors." For a week, local Okinawan citizens and politicians blocked off a main gate protesting the deployment of the Osprey tiltrotor aircraft to Okinawa. This was one of the more controversial aircraft that the US military operated. As of 2024, there have been about 400 Ospreys produced since 1988. From these, there have been thirteen crashes with more than fifty fatalities. This is why they protested. The locals didn't want it on their island in case it was as unsafe as they'd been told.

During the Osprey protests, I got a good history of the other incidents and the local outrage from one of the Japanese women who worked for us.

My second experience with the Okinawan activists happened a few months after I got to the island. Two sailors were accused of raping a local woman, and the following year, the two were convicted and sentenced to ten years in prison. After their arrest in 2012, the entire island was on lockdown to try to appease the activists and politicians. Every military member on the island had to be on base or in their home off base by 11 p.m. every night and couldn't leave until 5 a.m. During that time, I came to learn about some of the other high-profile sexual assault cases, including an incident in 1995 where two sailors and two marines were convicted of raping a twelve-year-old girl.

Needless to say, the activists and politicians did not like the US occupation of their home, where 50,000 US troops and their family members lived, occupying 15 percent of the island's land.

When we drove the ambulance to the gate, a local Japanese news station shoved their microphones through the windows along with their cameras, trying to get us to say something. We didn't, of course. The last thing we needed was to be on national TV giving comments on an incident when we still didn't know all the details.

We were led by a marine vehicle down some dirt roads to an opening in the jungle that was about two football fields wide and one football field long. The smoke was still about a half mile away coming from the side of the hill beyond the open field. In the football field was another ambulance and multiple firetrucks parked, waiting for orders, along with several other vehicles carrying high-ranking members who I had never seen before.

An Air Force colonel walked over to our ambulance. "Flight medicine?" Denson nodded. "We ain't getting in there today. Bio needs to clean it up first before you guys can start anything.

Lots of shit burning that we can't expose anyone else to," the colonel said.

"Does anyone need any medical attention?" asked the flight surgeon.

"Three of the passengers are stable. Fourth passenger hasn't been recovered. Pararescue is out there now. Stand by for the next hour in case we need you, then have your crew back tomorrow at zero seven hundred sharp and we can get you to the crash site to start the mishap investigation if bio clears up the area. This one might take a while. More tomorrow," the colonel said and walked away to direct another vehicle.

Denson gave me a look, and I knew what it meant. We didn't say a thing the entire drive back to base, and the news spread around all the way to the major media places in the states. We didn't know who the fourth passenger was, but it was surely one of our patients at the clinic.

The next morning we were back at 0700 sharp, and I could see smoke still billowing from the side of the hill, not as thick as the day before but still noticeable from across the island. We were instructed to park on the road leading to the open field because a Chinook chopper was scheduled to land within the next twenty minutes.

"Come on, we need to be out there for this," Denson said. I didn't know what was going on, but I followed his orders to the edge of the field.

Around forty military personnel from all branches working the crash site that morning made a single-file line around the open field. I could hear the Chinook coming. When it got close, we bent down to cover our faces from the dust kicked up by the helicopter's downwash. Once it had landed and the dust was clear, we stood and were instructed to face the smoky hillside and salute.

From the other end of the field I saw two heads peek up from the valley that the field dipped into before rising again into the hillside where the crash was. Then two more heads popped up after them, and two more, until I saw twelve airmen marching in formation in the field, two of the middle airmen carrying a box with an American flag draped over it. A thirteenth airman outside the formation gave them the orders. Giving the formation orders was one of the highest ranking enlisted airmen on the island, and arguably the best leader I ever crossed paths with while I served in the Air Force. He was a pararescueman, and he embodied what it meant to be selfless and a strong leader. I would find out later that these men, including this leader, had been out there on the fiery hillside since the crash the day before, trying to get the fourth airman. Their march up to the field was their first time out of the smoky jungle in almost sixteen hours. No sleep, no food, nothing.

As we held our salute, the fourteen men loaded onto the Chinook, and it flew away. We held the salute until the helicopter was gone. When the field cleared, the emptiness was as it was before, only I could feel it now. Only the sound of sniffles for a few moments after the Chinook left.

For the rest of that day, every person working in that field didn't say a word. We set up tents and the makeshift headquarters for the investigation and readied the field for what would end up being a several-week operation recovering every nut and bolt of the helicopter from the hillside. We were there almost every day.

Tech Sergeant Mark A. Smith was thirty years old.

MARCH 2012, COLORADO

While I was in Japan, Devin spent his days in Vail, Colorado. Like myself, Deev had his own way of working through everything. While I withdrew and distracted myself with books and movies, Devin found another way to deal.

When Devin first got to Colorado, he had already built a resume of coping gone bad, and I already knew he liked to tip back on some booze occasionally, although Colorado took it a step further.

Knock knock knock.

Devin opened the door of his apartment, and in front of him stood a long-haired hippy, mid-twenties, in a tie-dye headband and tattered clothes with a little white Maltese puppy in his arm. The puppy was just as haggard looking as the hippy holding him.

"Hey man, I found this. Is this your old lady?" the hippy said, handing Devin a piece of mail.

"Uh yeah, this is my girlfriend," Devin said, looking at the name on the piece of mail. "Where'd you find this?"

"It was on the street, man. And that was my sign to come here."

"Well, thanks. I appreciate it."

They stood looking at each other in an awkward pause, when finally Devin said to the complete stranger at his door, "You want something to eat?"

"Sure man! Call me Tree, by the way."

"Tree?" Devin asked, confused.

"Yep, Tree."

"All right, Tree, come on in." The two walked inside, and Devin made them soup and grilled cheese.

"Where are you from, Tree?" Devin asked.

"Home is wherever I am. I'm from nowhere," Tree said.

The conversation went like this for an hour. Devin would find out that Tree didn't have an age, he didn't have a real name, and he didn't have a family. Everything Devin asked him about was a "social construct and not important. It's only about love, man." While Tree was inside the apartment, he refused to look at any screen, especially the TV. Always having his back turned to it.

"It's evil. They want to brainwash you, man. Make you hate."

"Yeah, I guess that's true, but there's nothing wrong with *The Office* from time to time."

"You know, Devin, I live my life off of signs, and if everyone did the same, their life would be filled with love. That paper I found with Emma's name on it brought me here. You have a good aura, man. I'm supposed to be here."

"Right on, man," Deev said. As weird as the situation was, Deev didn't care. Devin was good at connecting with strangers with outlandish characteristics. His key to connecting to people was he would not only listen, he would also take a genuine interest in them, especially their flaws and biggest quirks. He recognized them in everyone and embraced the flaws and often the pain behind them. Whether consciously or subconsciously, people can sense it, and in return they liked Deev. The hippy named Tree was no different.

"Well, maybe the sign was for you to come here and have lunch and hang out with me then, because Emma is at work right now."

Breee, Breee, Breee.

Devin's phone vibrated, and he answered. It was Emma's mom, calling from across the country asking what the hell was going on with Emma. Apparently, she was in the hospital.

"Sorry, Tree, I gotta go. Emma is actually in the hospital right now. I have to get down there and see what's going on."

Devin and Tree left the apartment when Devin realized the car that he and Emma shared was in the shop and Emma had their shared bus pass.

"Shit, Tree, I don't have a way to get there."

"I got this man," Tree said with confidence. Tree walked up to the edge of the highway and looked toward oncoming traffic, a small puppy on one arm, and a thumb up toward the road on the other. Almost immediately a car stopped.

"Come on, bro, let's get to the hospital," Tree said as he entered the car. Devin didn't have a choice, and he followed.

Ten minutes later, the car reached the emergency room. Devin rushed to the front desk.

"I'm here to see Emma. She's my girlfriend. Her mom just called and said she was here," Devin said.

"Let me see what room she's in here," the nurse said, stopping herself and shifting her attention. "Sir, you can't have animals in here."

Devin looked behind him to see that Tree had followed him into the hospital and was standing next to him with his puppy.

Tree smiled and nodded at the nurse. "Okay, man, right on."

"She's in room 114, sir. You can head back, but he has to leave," the nurse said.

"Right on," Tree said smiling, beginning to head to the room.

"Sir!" the nurse called, immediately calling security, who then escorted Tree and his puppy out of the hospital.

At that point, Deev didn't even care about Tree. He just wanted to see if Emma was okay. He walked back to room 114, where she sat up in a hospital bed hooked up to an IV.

"Devin, oh my God, I couldn't get ahold of you. My mom called you?"

"Yeah, that's how I knew to come," he said.

"My phone died and I could only remember her number. I was riding the bus when all of a sudden I just blacked out. I don't even remember how I got here."

Devin would come to find out later that she had suffered a panic attack, likely fueled by a cocktail of pills she and Devin had been experimenting with for months beforehand, on top of gallons of booze a week.

Like Devin, Emma was in Colorado away from home to work and live a new life in a beautiful place. They'd met at a party and started dating shortly after.

"How did you get here without the car or the bus pass?" Emma asked.

Devin looked toward the door of the hospital room and there stood Tree with his Maltese puppy.

"Tree! What the hell, man? I thought security kicked you out?" Devin said.

"They didn't block the back door, man. Rules are for sheep, dude," Tree said.

"Emma, this is Tree. He stopped by the house earlier with a piece of mail he found with your name on it. That's when your mom called, and he hitchhiked us here."

After a few hours in the hospital, Emma was released, and they made their way back to the apartment, including Tree.

For the next few months, Tree would come and go from the apartment, usually when he needed food, and he would occasionally sleep on the floor, always with his back to the television. Tree had a snowboard that he would keep outside, and one day, when Devin asked him if he wanted to bring it inside for the night so nobody stole it, Tree said, "No man, if someone wants to borrow it, that's cool. Hopefully they put it back, but if not, that's cool too. It's just a thing."

The snowboard was eventually stolen and never returned.

After about two months of Tree coming and going, Devin asked about the signs he'd first mentioned. "So Tree, tell Emma about the signs you live your life by. Like if I were to hold this up right here"—Deev held up an orange—"that could be a sign to you, right? This orange is somehow the universe talking to you?"

Tree's eyes lit up like he had some sort of revelation, and without saying a word, he walked out of the apartment. The next morning he showed back up with a brown paper bag full of the worst types of food you can get from the food shelf, mostly canned beets and canned yams.

"This is for you guys, man. Thanks for showing me love and for feeding me. Here's some food to replace what I ate. There's not a lot of people like you in this world, and I love you for it."

"Well, thanks, Tree. Are you leaving or something?" Devin asked.

"Headed to Florida with these guys." Tree pointed to a van in the parking lot waiting for him. "Yesterday morning they invited me to go with them, I wasn't too sure about it and then yesterday afternoon you held up that orange. That was my sign, man. All I needed. I'm supposed to go to Florida."

That was the last time Devin would ever see the hippy named Tree, but that was not the last time people came and went from the apartment.

Every day, people would walk in unannounced looking for Emma, and the pills they wanted from her. Percocets, Vicodin, Oxys...you name it. It was the apartment to get them from.

Devin and Emma would go to their shifts at the restaurants where they worked, they'd come home, they'd get high, pass out, get up, and repeat the cycle. This went on for months until the day Devin decided to move back to Minnesota.

On that day, Devin came home from work and went through the normal routine. "Emma," he said. She got off work first and was usually already home waiting for him.

Nothing.

Devin walked back to the bedroom, and he saw Emma on the bed, presumably taking a nap. Devin tiptoed until he noticed her eyes were wide open.

"Emma?" He walked over to her and noticed a blue hue to her skin.

"Emma!" He touched her cheek trying to wake her up. "Oh my god."

Devin picked her up and brought her to the bathroom where he set her in the bathtub, turning on the water from the shower trying to stimulate her senses somehow. Her eyes were still open and her skin was getting more blue.

"Talk to me, Emma, talk to me," he said, splashing water on her face. "Please, Emma, talk to me!"

Nothing.

"EMMA!"

Cough Cough Cough

A single blink.

"Oh my god. Can you hear me? Hey!"

No direct response, but she was alive.

Devin rushed her to the hospital, where they learned she had overdosed.

Devin was sure he had just seen his girlfriend dead, and it was at that moment, he realized he needed to change something. The change he made was moving back to Minnesota, away from Emma and this toxic life they had created together. As Tree would say, this was his sign, and who knows how many signs he'd ignored before that?

They were easier to ignore in Colorado, but once back in Minnesota, the memories of Christmas Eve 2007 flooded back to Devin like a dam breaking. Seeing people he recognized, seeing places where memories were made, it was impossible to avoid thoughts of our dad. When thoughts of our dad started, soon followed memories of Christmas Eve in 2007. Once in motion, the movie had to play out in full. When this happened to me, I shut myself away from the world. I withdrew and rode it out alone. When this happened to Devin, he started drinking an entire liter of alcohol in a single day. For reference, a single liter of alcohol might be able to get an entire sorority drunk for weeks. For some people, a liter of alcohol in a day is enough to kill.

When Devin blacked out, the memories died, and when he figured this out, he started to rely on this method. It culminated in Devin not showing up to work one day. At noon, my uncle and his boss showed up to his place where he lived by himself and found him passed out on the floor, an empty bottle at his side.

Halfway around the world, I had no idea any of this was happening.

CHAPTER 9

"Sometimes you have to do things you don't want to do."

Dad used to tell Devin and me this before our wrestling matches when we were eight and nine. We would be nervous and say we didn't want to wrestle that day in order to avoid feeling that pre-match anxiety. At eight and nine, it was a nerve-racking experience. Every kid our age would show up at a gym in some small farm town in Minnesota. They would weigh everyone in and write your weight on your hand. Then, you would organize into a line with kids who were your same weight, and you would stand and assess your possible opponents. If you got a kid from Green Bush in your group, the nerves struck a little sharper. They were good. When we would go through this process, we hated feeling those nerves. We would tell our dad that, and he wouldn't let us back away from competing. It would have been a shame if we hadn't wrestled, because we were good at it. Dad knew this and pushed us to compete. He'd say, "Those butterflies in your stomach will go away once that first round starts." Sure enough, the first match would start, and the butterflies were gone. Afterward, we were thankful to follow through with the thing we didn't want to do, especially when we were holding onto a first-place medal. It was a common thing for us, especially Devin, on those weekends.

It is the best lesson Dad instilled in me. "Sometimes you have to do things you don't want to." It seems contrary to what kids are taught today, or at least what the mainstream message seems to be. Today we are not supposed to feel any amount of discomfort or anxiety, at least that's what we're told. If you're nervous or have an ounce of anxiety about work or your upcoming family event or anything at all, then something must be wrong with you and you need a pill for it...again, that's just what we're told.

"Put one foot in front of the other. Have confidence in yourself and the work you have done to be a good wrestler, and everything will work out how it's supposed to. You can do this," Dad would say. "You will be happy you did it when the day is over. I promise." And he was always right about it. To this day, I use those lessons to help me push through things, and it works.

I thought about this lesson as I sat in the doctor's office waiting room thinking about my "victim impact statement."

I didn't know what this was until the court proceedings neared in the fall of 2008. A victim impact statement is an oral or written statement for victims of a crime to speak during the court proceedings, oftentimes to tell the judge and/or jury how the crime has impacted them. I sat and thought about what I would say and how the hell I would get up there in front of a courtroom full of people and my dad and say my statement. This was my own father, and I had to stand in front of him and say how this all impacted me and my brothers and my mom. It seemed like an impossible task to do it and do it calmly, while still saying everything that needed to be said.

"Sometimes you have to do things you don't want to," I said to myself. "Man the hell up." The court proceedings hadn't even started yet, and it wasn't even a sure thing that any of us would have to give a victim impact statement—much was still to be decided—but I wanted to mentally prepare myself.

Another thing I didn't want to do was go to a therapist to "talk," but I did it, because Mom wanted all of us to.

"Desmond," the therapist said, calling me back to her office.

I walked in, and it wasn't what I expected a therapist's office to be like. I had never been to one, and I expected everything to be perfectly in order. I expected a super loud grandfather clock ticking in the background like in the movies and a Newton's cradle on the desk going "*click, click, click*" as the metal ball on each end swung back and forth. That wasn't how the office was at all.

This office had no file cabinets, but it needed one. Maybe ten. The office had about 1,000 manilla folders and another 10,000 loose sheets of paper scattered around the room. It was like *Hoarders: Office Space* edition.

"Take a seat, Desmond," the therapist said. I sat in the only open chair. The rest had stacks of folders on them. She was a short fat woman with gray hair and tiny glasses that barely covered the blacks of her eyes, and she sat on an exercise ball instead of an office chair. She spoke with a calming voice, but that was the only thing calming about her. I was only there because Mom wanted all four of us to see a therapist about everything we had experienced, not because I wanted to be there or even thought I needed help sorting out my feelings. I certainly didn't have an open mindset to "talk" with a complete stranger, and her first impression in the cluttered, claustrophobic office made me think she was actually the one who should be talking to someone, not me.

"So, Desmond, what do you want to talk about today?"

"What do you mean?" I said.

"What do you want to talk about?"

"Isn't that what you are supposed to decide? Respectfully, of course, I don't mean to sound rude. I just thought that I came here and answered a bunch of questions or something. I pick what to talk about?"

"I'm here to talk about whatever you want to talk about. That's it."

I was really confused, I didn't think this is how it would go at all.

"Okay. Ummm, well. Do you see lots of families like this?" I asked.

"Like what?"

"Like mine."

"What is your family like?"

You have to be kidding me, I thought.

When I got done with that day, I told Mom I'm absolutely not going back to waste my time with that lady again. The truth is I didn't want to see anyone. *I don't need to*, I thought. The situation with Dad was the situation in our lives, and we weren't going to change it. It sucked, but I had accepted it, and I didn't need a therapist to help me figure out how I felt. *I'm fine*, I told myself.

The next week, Mom had the four of us individually go to a new therapist. I was disappointed to see no kinetic balls or grandfather clock in the new office, either. This place at least didn't have a mountain of papers like the other one.

This lady was a little different as well. She seemed much more professional, but I still felt something artificial about her. She was older with short gray hair, and she started asking me questions right away about the night with my dad.

After about a half hour of talking, the therapist said, "You're not too into this therapy thing, are you?"

"No," I said, and that was the last time I ever saw a therapist.

It wasn't that I thought they were scam artists or that therapy was stupid. I truly thought, and still do, that it could help people if they had nobody else to talk to, but I had people to talk to. People I trusted. I had no idea who these therapists were, and I was supposed to just have a strong enough bond of trust with these strangers to share my life with them?

The truth is I wasn't dealing with any of it and should have kept searching for someone to talk to who I trusted. I began to withdraw slowly starting my senior year. Soon after the incident, it was easy to distract myself with baseball and football and girls. When I wasn't focused on any of those, my friends and I would hang out listening to music, make skits, or play games in our new basement. After the night with my dad, my brothers and I never set foot again in our old house. Mom's friends and our family all got together, packed up our house, and moved all of our belongings a mile down the road to a place we would move into about a month later. With our old house being just a mile away, and on the way to the public beach, you would probably guess that I would have passed by it all the time, but I didn't. Whenever I was meeting friends at the beach, I wouldn't take the direct path. Instead I took the turn onto Memorywood Lane and would go an extra mile out of the way to not have to pass the old house. Because when I did, I would start thinking about things. The one time I did pass the house, I saw the crooked shingles on our old garage, and for the rest of the day, I sat and thought about everything again, snowballing from one memory to the next.

I thought about that garage and how it had burned down a few years before, and when we rebuilt it, the garage sat unfinished for two years. Half the roof was shingled for those two years, and my dad kept saying he was going to finish it but never did. Finally, in the summer of 2007, after my dad moved to his apartment, my friends and I decided to shingle the remaining side. We had never done it before, but it seemed pretty simple and hard to mess up. When we were done, one of my best friend's dad, who knew all about roofing, came to inspect our job.

"Need to redo it," he said.

"Really?! I thought we killed it! What did we mess up?" I asked.

"Yeah, you guys can't be roofers for your career. Look at this. Look at how crooked you guys put these on!" He pointed to one side of the roof.

I shook my head and pointed to the other side. "No, we did this side."

"Who the hell did that side? Were they drunk?"

"My dad did," I said.

A few years earlier, I would have felt humiliated, but I was over that feeling. He wasn't wrong when he asked if whoever did it was drunk.

I thought about that whole scene when I drove by the old house. I thought about that Christmas Eve. I thought about the first time my mom and dad split up, and even though I was months removed from the event, I saw how easy it was to let my mind snowball if I let it. No more of that, I told myself. So instead, I avoided the house to avoid the snowballing.

The memory snowballing was impossible to avoid that fall once the court hearings started.

It was the beginning of the football season, and instead of focusing on my team and being a captain, which should have been one of the proudest things I had done up to that point, I was constantly thinking about my victim impact statement. What should I say? How do I tell this story to everyone in court? During that fall semester, when the court proceedings were supposed to start, I made sure I had the first hour open on my school schedule, which was awesome to sleep in, but I did it to avoid the social interactions in the mornings. I knew all of this garbage would be in the paper again at some point, and I didn't want to talk about it with anyone. So to avoid talking about it, I avoided people. I did the same for my lunch periods. I made sure to have an open hour that butted up against my lunch period, so I could leave school and not have to be with everyone during lunch. Another way I successfully avoided people.

I would show up for two classes in the morning, then go to lunch, then I would come back and have a gym class. Oftentimes I was able to skip that without any trouble. Classes each day seemed over in a flash, just how I wanted it.

Then, the first hearing occurred.

That morning, I had to check into the attendance office and make sure I got a note so I could miss my afternoon classes. I also made sure to tell my coach that I might be late for practice. Like Coach Hock, our head coach, Coach Stolski, had been there for me for a long time. The year after my parents first split up, he'd called me out of class one day to see how I was doing and to make sure I knew that he and the rest of the coaches were there if I needed them. Then, a few months after the incident, our church had a small benefit for my family to help cover some of the expenses my mom was facing with three teenage boys and now only one income. At church, during the benefit serving the food, was Coach Stolski. He served every last plate. He was there for us, and it meant more than I can say. That night, at least 300 people showed up. My mom cried seeing the amount of support we had, and in a very hard and desperate time, our community rallied around us.

Driving to the courthouse that afternoon, I didn't feel nervous, but I felt sick. Not nauseous, but the achy feeling you have when you get the flu. I couldn't believe that I was driving to a courtroom to sit in a court hearing about my own father trying to kill my mom. It still felt surreal when I *had* to sit and think about it.

"Sometimes you have to do things you don't want to," I said to myself. This is just what I have to do now. No feeling sorry for yourself. Just do it.

When we arrived, the courtroom was packed. It was mostly our family there to support my mom, brothers, and me. Beau didn't come—Mom thought he was too young—but Devin and I sat in the back row with our mom. Our other family didn't think it was a good idea if we sat any closer. I felt calm waiting for my dad to walk in, still a little achy.

The door opened on the right, and in walked a man with a shaved head and long goatee wearing an orange jumpsuit. It was my dad. I barely recognized him.

I watched him walk across the courtroom to the desk on the other side of the room where his lawyer sat.

I felt eyes watching Devin and me to see how we would react to seeing him. But there wasn't much of a reaction, at least not externally. I tried to remain as stone-like as I could, while my thoughts raced. I stared at the back of his head.

That's my dad. My dad is sitting there in an orange jumpsuit. How? Why?

I don't remember a single thing the judge said. I just sat there in my own head. When we left, I rushed back to the high school for football practice. I ran onto the field about forty-five minutes late.

"Janousek, you're late, man! Where were you?" asked one of the younger players.

"Family stuff," I said.

I didn't want to be at practice that day. Something I'd loved to do and be a part of was suddenly the opposite. I was one of our best players and had a chance to play in college, but I wanted none of it anymore. I was a leader on the team, and I had to show up every day and do my best, so I tried, but my mind and heart weren't there fully.

The one thing I began to do a lot, which seemed to help me, was write. Mostly a journal at first to try and sort out what I was thinking on days where I caught myself snowballing. I felt like I was writing messages to Grandpa and telling him about it all, hoping he'd share some advice with me. At that time, I wished he was still around to be there with my mom, brothers, and me. When I wasn't writing, I made videos with my brother and our friends. I also started making cartoons. It was my latest creative adventure. I made little stop motion animations on Post-it notebooks and figured out how to make stop motion cartoons on Windows Paint and Windows Movie Maker by creating an image, making it .16 seconds long (the shortest possible clip then), then slightly changing the next image to make it look like the characters were moving. They took forever to make, but when I was making them, my mind was 100 percent consumed. The end goal was making them funny enough to get my friends to laugh, which was the ultimate success. When my mind was consumed, the memory loop couldn't start. So I began making them in all of my free time.

At the same time, I was supposed to be thinking about colleges. At least that's what I was told by everyone around me. I hadn't applied to a single college yet, and I'd hated the only one I visited, which was in Wisconsin. That's where my mind was... stooping as low as attending college in Wisconsin! But seriously, the idea of college was not something I wanted. The problem was if I said that to my teachers or guidance counselors, they would say, "You're too smart not to go to college. It would be a big mistake if you didn't go." I did well in high school with my grades—I got around a 3.8 GPA—but a lot of this was in large part because I was forced to get good grades. I wanted to play sports, which required good grades to play. I didn't get good grades because I loved filling in bubbles on a test and learning about British literature and calculus. I hated it. I wanted to make movies and write my own stories. I knew there were film schools and creative writing degrees, but I didn't want to do that either at that time in high school. At the time, it seemed silly to go learn how to be creative. I knew how to make things already, and I just wanted to make them.

"Gotta go get a degree so you can go work in a cube for fifteen to twenty years to pay for that piece of paper, and then you'll be happy." It made no sense to me, and still makes no sense to me. Especially when unlimited knowledge is in the palm of everyone's hands now.

College didn't matter, football mattered very little that year, and overall, that fall was a blur. I just wanted high school to be done with, and in the heart of the football season, it got a little fuzzier when they started playing some of the 911 phone calls in court.

"We need the police. Please hurry," my voice played to the courtroom. Immediately my mind was back on Christmas Eve, reliving it.

I heard the door *slam*, the footsteps up the wooden stairs to our front door *DUMPF, DUMPF, DUMPF* and the *POUND, POUND, POUND* of his fist before I heard, "OPEN THE FUCKIN' DOOR! NOOOOOOOOW!"

CRASHHHHHHH the sound of glass from the window above me shattering... The rock-hard pit that was growing all day in my stomach exploded, and a tidal wave of adrenaline hit my heart. I jumped off the couch and ran toward the stairs.

"Call the cops!" Mom said as she ran to the back bedroom upstairs. My brothers and I ran down the stairs in the opposite direction. At that moment, I felt like I was on autopilot. The only thing I knew I had to do was get away from my dad and call for help.

In what felt like a flash, I was in my room putting my shoes on and crawling out of the egress window out into the snow, following my emergency escape plan. While I was sprinting through the house and out the window I was pulling out my

Razor flip phone and dialing 911, waiting for the dispatcher. In a ring, they answered, "911, what's your emergency?"

"We need the police. Please hurry. We're on Clearwater Road."

As I was giving them our address, my mind came back from its tunnel vision mode of "run," and I realized I was standing in the woods behind our house. My body was in flight mode, and I had somehow made it all the way to the woods, about 200 yards away from my window, shin deep in snow.

"Police are on the way," the dispatcher said.

I looked back toward the house.

"Mom," I said.

I saw Devin and Beau crawl out of my basement window and run around the side of the house to the back patio on the other end of the house.

I met my brothers at the back door where we could see our shining Christmas tree from the back door window. Beyond the tree was the front window through which Dad had thrown a wooden chair from the front deck. Glass laid shattered everywhere on the couch where I had just been sitting a few moments before.

"I called the cops," I said to my brothers. We could hear the sirens in the distance.

"We have to go back inside," Devin said.

I reached for the backdoor handle. Locked.

I turned and looked down at Beau and saw that he wasn't wearing any shoes. He was standing on top of ice and snow in a pair of hole-filled socks.

I slid my size eleven brown Payless specials off my feet and put them on Beau's. When I put my socks onto the snow I felt nothing. My body was completely numb.

"I'm going back in," Devin said.

"Wait," I said. I reached into my pocket, pulled out the hunting knife, and handed it to Devin. Without hesitation, Devin grabbed it from me and sprinted in the direction of the egress window we'd crawled out of. I brought Beau around to the front of the house, in the opposite direction where the sirens were getting louder. The police were close.

I walked up to the front door to go back inside. I reached for the handle and turned it. Locked. The chair he'd used to shatter the window was on the front porch, as well as glass shards all over. His truck was still running in the driveway, headlights lighting up the shattered window.

Around the corner, the police lights lit up our driveway. Two police officers ran to us and I realized I had my keys in my pocket. I gave them to one of the officers who immediately went inside the house. A third officer showed up and took Beau and me to his squad car and put us in the back seat.

"I knew he would do this. I knew it," I said to myself.

Beau sat next to me, quiet. We watched, waited, for Mom to come out of the house.

"It's going to be okay, Beau. Mom's gonna be okay. Devin will be okay." I sat and I prayed that would be true.

I got back to the football locker room late for practice again. I didn't want to run down to the field.

"Sometimes you gotta do things you don't want to," I said aloud, trying to get my mind right. It felt like walking through mud some days, slogging my way through the motions. I knew I had to do it, but each step felt heavier and heavier.

I got home that evening, and right when I walked in, Mom told me that there wasn't going to be a trial. Facing second-degree attempted murder charges, my dad could have spent more than twenty years in prison. Instead, the lawyers agreed to first-degree assault causing great bodily harm, which carried a sentence "no greater than twenty years."

This meant no victim impact statement.

Part of me was relieved. Part of me was disappointed.

After all the mental preparation, I'd wanted to get up in front of the court and tell the judge and *him* what he'd done to us. Because of what he'd done, Mom required multiple surgeries to fix her face. Because of what he'd done, we had to go to school with a giant weight around our necks and pretend everything was normal. Because of what he'd done, we didn't have our father at home anymore. As much as I hated him when he was drinking, I needed him. I needed my dad, and because of what he'd done, I didn't have him anymore.

I felt so much anger, while at the same time relief that the court stuff was over. Relieved that we didn't have to deal with it anymore, and anger for having spent so much time building myself up for my victim impact statement.

I did not attend any of the further court proceedings. I don't even know how many more there were or how they went. Once I found out that I didn't have to make a statement, I wanted to feel normal and love football and school again and just move past it all.

Everything that happened in the courts thereafter I heard about through my mom. Dad was sentenced to one hundred months in prison, a little more than eight years, and he would only serve a part of it. He was eventually released in 2013, when I was in Japan. After he was sentenced, I avoided the newspapers. I wanted to just not think about it at all. Part of me was shocked that that's all the time he received.

For a while after he went away, I thought things would magically get better, but that wasn't true. I started avoiding everything social and was only hanging out with a handful of friends who I trusted. I finished the football season and tried to figure out what I wanted to do the next fall with college. By November, I had visited one more college in Duluth, and again, I didn't want to go there. I didn't want to go to college at all. I thought maybe trying to play football would make me want to go, but I didn't want to play football anymore.

In 2009, during the spring of my senior year, I played baseball and had one of the worst years I ever played. I was voted captain by my teammates, but I batted ninth and struck out more than anyone on the team that year, something I'd never done before. I was always one of the best hitters, but that year, my mind was not where it needed to be. My confidence all around was at an all-time low.

At the end of the school year was prom and the all-sports banquet where every team would come together to celebrate the letter winners, give out awards, and honor the senior athletes. That year, the media team made a highlight video, and the entire reel revolved around a kick return touchdown I'd had. It showed me running down the field and would flash back and forth to other highlights of other sports. It ended with me in the end zone with my teammates holding up a "number 1" and the reel fading to black. I didn't see this highlight, because I skipped going to the all-sports banquet, as well as my senior prom.

I had begun withdrawing more and more, but the entire time, I assured myself that I was just fine.

I just wanted to get out of high school and away from everyone and everything that had to do with that town. Finally, I decided on attending a private school called St. Thomas with one of my best friends in St. Paul, about two hours from Brainerd.

When I got to campus, I had an amazing time. I was forced to be social, which was one of the best things for me at the time, even though I didn't know that's what I needed. It would last for only two semesters, and not because I didn't want to keep going there. I loved that school and the people and I excelled in my classes. I got a 3.2 my freshman year, but I would have had to sell my soul to afford another three years.

I had $3,000 saved up from my summer job. I was able to get around $2,000 in small scholarships for tuition. I just assumed, based on what my teachers, counselors, and friends said, that if you signed a piece of paper the rest of the money you needed would be given to you as a loan.

That's when I learned that was not the case at all.

After the fall semester ended and spring rolled around, I found myself $4,000 short on tuition for the spring semester. There were no more loans, grants, and scholarships for me, and I realized I had only one more option.

My last option was to ask Dylan and Chase's dad for a loan. When I called Doug and told him my situation, he didn't skip a beat. "Yep, I'll loan you the money. It's a good investment. It'll be the only zero-percent loan you'll ever get." And Doug wrote me a check for $4,000. I couldn't have been more grateful for him, and still am. A few years later I wrote him a check to pay him back in full, with a 3 percent annual interest added on.

After I brought that check to the financial office at school, I walked back to my dorm room thinking, "Is this what I'm going to have to do every single semester? What about when I get out of college with all of this debt piled up?" It stressed me out and seemed incredibly irresponsible. How the hell was I allowed to have this student debt in the first place when there was no guar antee I could pay it back in the future?

I calculated what I could make with two full-time jobs that following summer, what I could make with a full-time job during college, and the numbers still didn't add up to what I needed. There was no possible way for me to cover it. My other option was to switch schools and go to a more affordable public school, but I loved where I was and didn't want to start fresh again at a new place.

For weeks I sat on it. During that time I went with a group of friends to look at a place to stay right off campus for the next year. After our visit, we all decided it was the place we wanted to stay during our sophomore year, and it would have been an absolute blast, but when it came time for me to write my name on the lease with the rest of the guys and hand over the first month's rent, I couldn't do it. I knew it wasn't the right decision. I didn't know what exactly I wanted to do for work after college, and stressing about finding more loans while working full time and doing classes sounded like a miserable and terrible decision. Then, considering the stress of making good on that mountain of student debt after I got done with school…I was stressed thinking about the future stress. Even with everyone around me telling me I was doing the right thing at school, I felt it wasn't. Right then and there, I decided I was done with college at St. Thomas. It was a hard decision but the responsible one. I felt a sense of relief but a new question arose: "Now what?"

There was about a month left of school, and I was still holding on to threads of hope that I'd show up at my mailbox one day to find an unexpected scholarship or grant awaiting me, even though I hadn't applied to any that I hadn't already heard back from. I pathetically showed up with hope every morning to the mail room with that delusion, only to leave with disappointment. Finally, one morning, I did have a letter in my mailbox, but it wasn't a scholarship or anything to do with school. It was a piece of mail with the top torn open already, addressed to me with the return address showing, "NOTICE - Mailed from a MN correctional Facility."

I froze. I could not compute what I was holding. For almost eight months, I had been distracted with friends, parties, girls, and school, and my mind was in a completely different place. A good place. Everything with my dad I had tucked away nice and neat in a box in the far back corner of my memory space, not touched in that entire time I was at school. Now holding this letter, that box got ripped open, and I was facing everything I had tucked away nose to nose. I stood holding the letter for five minutes when I realized I looked like a frozen zombie. I walked out into the foyer of the campus building and found a seat. I sat and stared at the envelope as people came and went. I ran through the memories that I hadn't touched in months as I tried to decide what I wanted to do with this letter. Do I read it? Do I throw it away?

Part of me felt angry that he would send me a letter. I was doing so damn well, not thinking about any of this crap for months, and now he was forcing me to deal with it again. On his terms, not mine. A small ounce of me was also happy. I wanted to tell my dad everything about my new school, about the girl I was dating, about Devin visiting my campus and getting tackled by a security guard... The good side of my dad would have been so proud of me for my good grades and good decisions and laugh with us at some of the stupid things we did... Then I would remember that I was leaving my school because of a terrible financial spot he'd left our family in. I would remember when he wasn't there for me when I needed him most during my senior year. I would remember what he did that night after he'd told us he was going to get better at rehab. This anger-to-happy cycle played out in my head back and forth as I held the envelope until I realized I had been sitting there for three hours, trapped in my own head with my thoughts.

I thought about stowing the letter away without reading it, but I knew it would sit there and tear at me and consume me until I opened it, so I saved myself the angst and finally did.

It was a handwritten page front and back, in pencil.

"I am very proud of you and I cannot begin to tell you how much I love you and miss you. Along with Devin and Beau. It is said that tears are the language of angels, I have been talking to them a lot. I have made many poor choices that have devastated the lives of many. Which there are no excuses for. I was wrong for so many things. I hope and pray that everyone is well..."

The letter went on, but I couldn't keep going.

Screw you, I thought. *Screw you for making me read this right now.*

I was so angry...and I was so happy. I kept going back and forth. I loved so much about my dad when he was being a good dad. Seeing him write "I am very proud of you" reminded me about all of the good things. About him teaching me how to play sports, about him teaching me how to hunt and clean a deer, about him teaching us how to manage and battle through our emotions in wrestling. I missed that dad so much, and then I would look at the envelope again and see the "MN Correctional Facility" label and be reminded of all the bad things he did. Driving us to the orthodontist higher than a kite, his rage when I pissed the bed, and that Christmas Eve night.

Without reading the rest of the letter, I began folding it up and putting it back in the envelope when I dropped a second form from the envelope. I picked it up and saw he had included a "visiting privilege application" form.

"Screw you," I said aloud. *You expect me to come visit you?*

I was even angrier. I put the letter back in the envelope and walked back to my dorm room.

The truth was I was mad at him because I felt like he was forcing me to forgive him, and at the time, I hadn't even forgiven myself yet. Whenever I thought of Christmas Eve 2007, I thought about everything I did wrong that night and what I should have done differently. First, I should have never even let my mom and brothers and I go home. I knew what was going to happen. I felt it. Second, the instant my dad broke in, I shouldn't have ran and called the police for help. I should have stayed in the living room and took him on, even if he would have crushed me like a bug and killed me. He would have hurt me instead of my mom. And third, I should have never given Devin the knife. I should have told Devin to give Beau his shoes and bring him around to the front while I went inside.

I'd failed on so many levels that night, I reminded myself, and I hated myself for it. Every bit of confidence in myself that I had built back up that year at college was suddenly gone.

When I got back to my dorm room I went into my closet. I dug into the very back corner and pulled out my grandfather's gray metal box. I put the letter from my dad in it, put the box back in the closet, and wouldn't open it again for almost three years.

CHAPTER 10

It had been weeks since the helicopter crash, and every morning we were still showing up to the Marine Base to assist with the investigation. We would arrive in the mornings, several different crews would be there with different missions, and we'd walk a trail through the hilly jungle up to the crash site. Like most of my military experience, most of our time was spent hurrying up and waiting. Over those next few weeks, I spent a lot of time sitting at the top of a little jungle mountain with Denson, looking down at burnt-up forest and a debris field of the crashed helicopter.

We hardly said a word to each other. In a weird way it felt like I was back home fishing with my buddies. Sometimes on the lake you just sit and enjoy being out there, even if you're not catching anything, hours of not saying a word to each other. In this case, we were sitting in this beautiful weather on a beautiful island, but the beauty was overshadowed by what had happened there a few weeks earlier. It was symbolic in a way—in one place there was both beauty and horror, and you could choose to see whichever you wanted.

One day, we got back from the crash scene, and my mom wanted to get on a phone call. She had me worried when I got her text asking to jump on a call. It would have been around 4 a.m. her time, and if it couldn't wait until our weekend call, then it must be something important. Hopefully not bad.

"Hey, what's going on? Why did you want to call? It's early there," I said.

"Yeah, it's super early. I just wanted to check in and see how things were going with you," she said.

"That's it?" I asked as I exhaled a sigh of relief. "I thought something was wrong. You have never called during the week like this."

"No, nothing is wrong, I just wanted to make sure you were doing okay with everything going on with your dad."

"What do you mean?" I asked.

"Him getting out of prison today. I just wanted to make sure you were doing okay. Just wanted to check on you, that's all."

Holy shit, I thought. *I forgot he was getting out.* From Christmas Eve 2007 when he was arrested to 2013 when he was released, he served roughly sixty-six months of his term and was released early for good behavior.

"I'm doing fine, Mom. Thanks for checking on me. Are you guys doing okay?"

We talked for a few more minutes, and when I hung up, my mind was racing. I started the memory snowballing again. Then I started thinking about my mom's and my brothers' safety. Would he try to find them? Would he try to contact any of us?

In my dorm room under my bed, I pulled out the gray metal box and found the letter. I hadn't looked at it for years. I sat and stared at it until it got dark. Would he be pissed that I didn't go see him? If so, would he go find my mom again? I went to bed, but I just laid there with my eyes closed until my alarm rang. I didn't actually fall asleep that night.

When I showed up to the ambulance the next morning, Denson was already waiting, ready to go to the crash site.

"You look like shit," Denson said to me.

"Thanks, so do you," I said.

He laughed, and we began the drive to the Marine base in silence.

That day, the wife of the airmen who'd lost his life in the crash was at the site. I didn't see it, but at the site, she allegedly left a cross and her and her husband's wedding rings. She sobbed and said goodbye to her husband. Afterward, she thanked the recovery crew and left. I thought about this woman and everything she must have been feeling. In absolute agony, mourning. Shattered. One of her pillars, gone. Her kids' pillars.

On the drive home, Denson broke the silence between us. "That really messed you up, huh? That lady out there?"

"My dad got out of prison yesterday," I said. The last thing I wanted to do was talk about it, but I couldn't take it anymore. I had to tell someone.

"Fuck," Denson said. "Well, that explains a lot."

After a few moments of awkward silence, he asked, "You ever box?"

"Never, but I was in wrestling and karate growing up."

"Well, it's a little different, but let's box later. Meet me at the gym."

Back at the base, I ran to my dorm to grab some workout clothes and met Denson at the gym. We grabbed one of the racquet ball courts to use as our gym, and he started showing me how to put wraps on my hands, and I put on the gloves.

"All right, we're going to shadow box. I need to see what I'm working with here. We're not going full speed yet."

We started shadow boxing, which was pretty much boxing without actually hitting each other. He pretended to punch me and watched my footwork as I moved out of the way and fake punched him back.

"Not bad. You probably ain't gonna punch through wet tissue paper until we fix a few things, but you're athletic. This isn't bad. It's good, honestly. Potential."

We went through a few more drills, each about three minutes just like a boxing round. By the tenth round, I was dying. I was in the best shape of my life, but this was a different kind of endurance.

"All right, let's see if you can take a punch."

"What?" I asked.

"We're going to box. Punch me as hard as you want."

I put on headgear, Denson didn't, and he rang the proverbial bell.

He jabbed me a few times, and I hit him back with a few body shots.

"Come on, remember the drills we just did."

He came at me, and I torqued my hips and threw a right hook that hit him square in the jaw. He stumbled backward and shook his head. He looked dazed for a few seconds before he snapped out of it. A smirk grew on his face.

"All right, that's not bad. Now, my turn."

Without skipping a beat, he threw a combination of punches back at me, hitting me square in the nose, turning it into a faucet of red. I saw stars, but when they wore off, I was pissed. To stop his barrage of punches, I went at him even harder. The rage I felt in my punches. I dug deep and thought of my dad. Swinging as hard as I possibly could with each punch, using up every ounce of energy I had left, and he could sense the rage. I hit him in the body a few times, but none hit square.

"Hey, hey, Janousek. Nope, nope. Stop. You lost your anchor. You're losing it right now, and that's how you turn into a punch-drunk dipshit in the ring. You'll get yourself killed like that."

He stopped me and stopped the round, my nose gushing blood, my heart about to explode after my rage-filled counter offense.

"What the hell? You keep saying this crap, 'Have an anchor.' Stop saying it unless you're going to explain it to me." I was still pissed.

"You lost your cool. I flipped your switch, and you let the rage take over. You lost your anchor in the ring. As soon as you start playing into your emotion, or letting your emotion play you, rather, you're done for. This is why boxing is an art. A lot of people see it as a stupid cock fight of who can hit each other the hardest until someone gets knocked out, but it's a chess match. I flipped a switch, and you flipped the board. You gotta harness that and control your emotions if you're going to box."

He tossed me a towel for my nose, and I sat and leaned against the wall, still trying to gain my breath. He sat across from me on the other wall.

"Remember when I told you my wife was Pentecostal?" he asked.

"Yeah," I said. "Is she still going to church or what?"

"I lied. She cheated on me."

"Well, I feel like an idiot then. I knew that was the case... Sorry man," I said.

"Nope. I lost my anchor. I got fat as fuck, and I didn't give her what she needed. It was my fault."

"Is that why you hate when people try to get out of their PT tests with profiles?" I asked.

"I'm trying to help them. I've been there. I let myself go, and it wasn't fair to my wife. I got too far removed from my purpose, which should have been her. I got fat and apathetic, and I lost her. I was a loser. I talk to people like I do, because it sucks. But it's all right. She deserves better than the piece of shit I was, and I truly hope she gets it."

"Who was the dude she cheated on you with?"

"My neighbor. I went to beat the piss out of him, and he wouldn't come out of his house. Probably a good thing I got deployed. Green Beret too. That little pussy."

We sat there for a few minutes, and I finally got my nose to stop bleeding.

"I don't know what the hell happened with your dad, and frankly, I'm not a therapist, so don't treat me like one, pouring your heart out to me. If there's one thing I can say to you, though, without me shoving a boot up your ass like all the fat turds we see, is: have an anchor. Find out what your purpose is, and don't forget it. When you do forget your anchor, that's when you start drifting into rough waters. There's something in you driving you. I don't know what it is, but stick to it, and you'll be fine." He stood up from the other side of the court, grabbed his gloves and the gloves I was using, and started to leave. "I'll see you tomorrow morning." And he left.

I sat there thinking about what he'd said about having an anchor, a purpose. That phrase finally made sense.

What is my purpose? I thought. It's something I'd never really defined for myself. *Why am I doing what I am doing in everything with my life?*

That evening, I went to dinner with the girl I was seeing. I wanted to share so badly with her the story about my dad, but I didn't want to change anything or make her think differently about me. I knew once I started talking about it she would see another side of me that she hadn't seen yet. So instead of talking about it, I bottled it up again. Throughout the next few years, on any date when I was asked about my parents, I simply lied and told them my dad was a machinist. It wasn't a total lie—that was what my mom's boyfriend (now husband) did. But I would leave out the part about my real dad. It was just easier for both of us, I told myself.

I had four months left in Japan when I found out that I'd be transferring bases back to San Antonio, to Lackland Air Base. I was excited to be back in the states and in the same time zone as home, but also a little disappointed that I'd be back in a place I already knew. I was leaving such a beautiful island and maybe never coming back again.

During my final months in Japan, I continued to write and create videos. It consumed all of my free time. I also had a stack of about a hundred books that I had read, and I had a few more I wanted to finish before everything got packed up and sent stateside to my new base. Aside from my writing, reading, and working out, I was consumed with defining my purpose.

What is my purpose?

I thought about the important people in my life growing up like my mom and Grandpa. What drove them? That answer was their family. Their purpose was providing for and raising their families. Being strong for them and being there for them.

My purpose, I concluded, was being the best father I could possibly be one day. Being better than my own father and giving my future kids everything I possibly could emotionally and providing for them financially. I was more driven than ever to achieve my dreams of writing and filming things that people would enjoy, and hopefully in turn, use my career to provide for the future family and community.

That was my purpose. That was my anchor. I just needed to find them.

CHAPTER 11

"Make sure you watch him. Don't let him out of your sight," Dad said to me.

We were at my uncle Tron and aunt Kelly's in the spring-time, and I wanted to play outside in the woods and bring Beau with me. He had turned two that January, so he could keep up with me walking, but like any two-year-old, he walked with a waddle and wanted to get into everything he saw. I was just about to turn eight in May and we were moving from Duluth to Brainerd. While we were waiting to move into the trailer park, our aunt and uncle let us stay in their fifth-wheel camper. I loved staying at Tron and Kelly's for the few weeks that we did. To me, it was a version of the farm back in Thief River Falls, just without the animals and equipment. They lived south of Brainerd down a long dirt driveway, at least a quarter mile, and as you drove through the trees and onto the property a giant pond appeared on your left. The driveway wrapped around the pond, and at the end of it was their trailer house. From the house, you couldn't see a neighbor anywhere, and maybe couldn't even hear a neighbor yelling at the top of their lungs. It was peaceful, and there was a lot to do outside, which I loved.

Where we were moving from in Duluth was much different than Tron and Kelly's. We lived in a part of Duluth down the street from an area called Morgan Park. Duluth overall has the highest rate of poverty in the state, but the Morgan Park area rate is slightly higher. The neighborhood was originally started as a community for the steel company workers. Duluth, along with most of northeast and north central Minnesota, boomed in the mid-1900s with the iron ore mines and the steel companies. Duluth was the major port for these mining companies, and the area flourished. Today, when you go to towns like Eveleth, you ask yourself, "How the hell does a small town like this have the Hockey Hall of Fame in it?" Because decades ago, it was home to a legendary hockey culture, in large part due to the thriving economy. With the economy, the schools were triple the student body sizes that they are today. But as the years passed, the mines shut down, and today most of these cities are just a few steps short of becoming ghost towns, a shadow of their former selves.

When the steel company shut down in Duluth, the Morgan Park housing was no longer needed for the steel workers, and it became a cheap place for families to move to. This is the area we lived in Duluth, in a 900-square-foot, two-bedroom palace. My mom and dad had one room and my brothers and I shared the other room. The houses were cramped into the neighborhood, but the best part about all the houses jammed in there were all of the kids who lived in our neighborhood. We had a little army of six-to-eight-year-olds running the place. It's where I learned how to ride a bike, lost my two front teeth, and where Devin and I earned our white belts in karate. We had a kid in our neighborhood whose dad was a carnival worker, and in the summer, he brought home a ride that he parked in the open lot and we all got to take turns riding the little tilt-a-whirl-like ride. We loved it there in Duluth. But I loved being at Tron and Kelly's in the countryside more.

Living in the country and going outside to do whatever we wanted in the woods whenever we wanted. We could shoot our BB guns, we could throw rocks as far as we could into the pond, or we could build a fort. Anything. It was amazing.

I took Beau with me outside and told him, "Follow me. Do not leave my side."

He looked at me like he understood, but I couldn't tell for sure. I tried to decide what adventure I was going to take us on. The possibilities were endless. I looked over at Kelly's garden. It seemed like the size of a small grocery store. It was gigantic. We could go over there and dig for worms or grubs, those things loved that black soil. I looked over at the pond and the island in the middle of it. We could try to venture out onto the island, but I decided against it because I had Beau with me. I didn't want to try and get him in and out of the canoe, and the last thing I wanted was to have him fall in. I'd be in deep trouble with my dad if that happened. A few years later, my cousins and I would go out to the island, and I would proceed to step on a wasp nest. I would get stung more than twenty times before I jumped into the water. I was fine, thankfully, but the next time I got stung, I would be allergic. My body was apparently shocked into never wanting another sting again.

Instead of the garden or the island adventure, I decided Beau and I would just take a stroll down the dirt driveway. I knew that during the summertime the turtles would plant their eggs in the dirt. It was a little early in the year to find turtle eggs, but I didn't know that, so I would take us on an egg hunt that day. Who knew what else we would find? I'd seen beavers, deer, skunks, and even bears. I carried a stick with me just to make sure I was prepared in the event we had to fight one off. As a worry wart, I always had to be prepared. The only thing I couldn't protect us from was a skunk spray. If one of those little stinkers got us, we would have to bear the stink, but I was willing to gamble to try and find a few eggs.

As we walked down the dirt driveway, I had to remind Beau a few times to "keep up." As the older brother, I had to make sure I whipped him into shape. He had to listen to me, I reminded him. "Stay right by me," I said.

As we were walking down the road, I saw a little hole in the driveway ahead.

"Turtle eggs, Beau!"

I ran over to the hole and started digging. I got down a few inches. No eggs. A few more inches. No eggs.

"Dang it!" I said. "False alarm."

I realized while I was digging that I'd lost track of Beau. I stood up from the hole and looked around for him. I couldn't see him.

"Beau!" I yelled. I started panicking. "Beau, where the heck are you!?"

I spun around and looked toward the pond, about twenty yards away from where I was standing on the driveway, and there he was. Face down in the water, arms and legs out like starfish as he was floating away from the shore line.

I ran down into the water and jumped in, water up to my knee, and grabbed him by the ankle, dragging him back to shore and out of the water.

COUGH COUGH. Beau spit up water and started sobbing. He sat on the shore with every inch of him soaking wet. I took his coat off and gave him my dry jacket. Luckily for him, it was in the forties, but even then, you didn't want to be outside when you're soaking wet at those temps. Growing up in Minnesota and playing outside all of the time in the snow, you learn fast the dos and don'ts of the cold.

"What were you doing?" I scolded him.

I was relieved that I'd saved him and I wasn't responsible for the drowning of my little brother, but I knew what was waiting for me when I got back to the camper. My dad was going to be pissed. He'd told me to watch Beau, and for just a minute I didn't, and it almost turned out to be a disaster. We walked back down the dirt driveway. The whole way back, Beau cried, and as much as I wanted to scold him more, it wouldn't change anything. Besides, he clearly knew he'd screwed up. I didn't need to hammer him anymore.

My heart was racing when we got back to the camper. Partially because my brother just almost died and partially because of the consequences I was about to face. I opened the door, and there was Dad, his face scrunched. He must have heard my brother crying.

"What the fuck is going on?!" he growled.

"Beau fell in the pond," I said, eyes on the ground.

"You were supposed to fuckin' watch him!" He grabbed the back of my neck with his claw and spanked me until I cried.

I knew other kids got spanked, but as I laid there and cried, I wondered why I had just gotten in so much trouble. I did in fact watch out for my brother. Had I just left him to fend for himself, he'd be dead. He would have drowned had I not pulled him out of the pond, and I got punished for saving him. He got wet, yes, but I watched over my little brother. I did. I knew I did.

Walking on eggshells was the norm, and after that, I was hyper cautious about what I did around Dad and what kind of repercussions everything carried. One wrong step on a creaky floor board could spark an ass whooping, and I hated ass whoopings. So I did whatever I could to make sure we avoided them.

"Hello?" Grandma said.

"Grandma...Dad hurt mom," I said. I didn't know how else to say it.

There was a second of silence. "...What?! Why? WHY?! Oh my god!"

I had to stay calm and try to keep Grandma calm. "Grandma, I need you right now. Please stay calm. I don't know what to do."

"We are on our way," Grandma said.

I sat with Beau in the back of the squad car and watched as two ambulances pulled up the end of our driveway.

I called our family friends Dan and LaCoe who lived down the street, less than half a mile away. "LaCoe, something bad happened. I don't know what to do right now, and you guys are the only ones I could call besides my grandma and uncles." In less than two minutes Dan and LaCoe were standing outside the window of the squad car. On Christmas Eve, they dropped everything to come to our side. I could only talk to them through the car window, and we didn't say much, but having them there with us was the most important thing.

I watched as Dan and LaCoe spoke with some police officers and tried to help us figure out what was going on. The whole time, we all watched the house and waited. I prayed and prayed as hard as I could that I would see Mom and Devin walk out okay.

"God, please. Please let Devin and Mom be safe. Please. Grandpa, if you're there, please be with them right now. Please." Over and over in my head.

The first person out was Devin. He was handcuffed. A police officer walked him to the back of a separate squad car.

Why the hell is my brother handcuffed? I thought.

I tried to get a police officer's attention to ask him, but they ignored me through the glass.

The second person out was Mom, and she was walking, barely. She was aided by two EMTs, one on each side of her, and she was holding a cloth on her face. I couldn't see her face, but I knew she was alive, and that's all that mattered. They put her in an ambulance and drove away.

Finally, Dad came out rolled on a stretcher. I had no idea what had happened with him and frankly didn't care. All I cared about was that Devin and Mom were okay, but I wanted to know more.

"What's going on?" I said to one of the officers who opened the door to talk with us.

"They'll talk to you guys more at the police station," he said.

"Can I get some shoes for my brother first?" I asked. The adrenaline was wearing off, and my feet started to feel the icy cold from my now sopping-wet socks. The officer brought a pair of shoes for Beau, and Beau gave me back my shoes.

LaCoe and Dan were still there outside the car.

"Your grandma and uncles are on the way, Tron is going to meet you at the police station, and you will stay with them tonight. Your mom is going to be okay. I love you guys so much," LaCoe said.

We said goodbye, and Beau and I were driven to the Brainerd Police department where an investigator was waiting for us to ask us about what had happened that night. We were brought into the station and sat down in what seemed to be a break room. They asked us if we wanted anything to drink or eat, then the investigator brought us back to a room separately to ask us questions. My mind raced the entire time. We had no idea what had happened *in* the house, we had no idea what was going on with our mom or Devin, and I needed to know.

The investigator talked to me first.

When I went into the room with him, the first thing I asked was, "Where is my brother Devin?"

"He's talking to one of the other officers right now," the investigator said.

"Is he in trouble or something? Why was he in handcuffs?"

"We're trying to figure everything out right now. The most important thing is I need you to tell me everything about tonight."

So I told him everything. I told him about my dad's strange texts, and when I said that, the investigator took my phone as evidence. I told him how I knew it was going to happen, because I felt something wasn't right with him. I told him how I'd grabbed the knife before leaving for his apartment and how when we got there, I saw the bottles and empty prescriptions, and I decided to remove us from the situation. I told him how I didn't want to go home, because I knew this was going to happen. I told him how, when we got home, he broke into the house, and we all ran outside. That's where I proceeded to give Beau my shoes and I gave

Devin the knife, and he went back inside through the window we'd escaped from.

After I talked with him, he brought Beau into the room for about twenty minutes. As Beau was in there giving his account of the night, I sat alone in the police station break room. No phone, just a TV playing *A Christmas Story* and my own thoughts swirling. It's hard to explain what a dreamlike state is if you haven't experienced it. Something so surreal is happening that you're sure you're dreaming. I sat there in disbelief.

This is our life. It's really happening like this right now. Like for real? I kept wondering. *Why?*

I looked up at *A Christmas Story*. I kept forgetting it was Christmas Eve.

Beau finally joined me in the waiting room. The investigator left us there, and a few minutes later Devin joined us. I was relieved to see him.

"What happened?" I asked him.

Devin shook his head. "He wouldn't stop."

I didn't press any further. I knew what he did.

Through a glass window in the break room, I saw my uncle Tron and cousin Aaron standing in the doorway of the police station.

The investigator walked us through the station and told us we would hear more from them in the coming days. We got in the car with Tron and Aaron and drove to their trailer house in the countryside. Once there, Grandma, Uncle Brent, and Aunt Cassandra (Brent's wife), and all of my cousins were there waiting for us. Grandma hugged us the second we walked in the door.

Later, my aunt Kelly made us some snacks and made sure we were squared away with blankets and pillows to sleep on the living room floor. Our entire family, fourteen of us besides Mom and Dad, were jammed into the trailer that Christmas Eve. As I laid beneath the Christmas tree that night, the shock wore off, and my body and mind were more exhausted than they'd ever been.

The next morning my uncles went to the hospital to be with Mom. They didn't want us boys to see her quite yet in the shape she was in. In the hospital, they put Mom in one room, and just down the hall was my dad who was getting treated for a punctured lung from where the knife got him.

My uncle Brent told me that he'd started walking over to my dad's room, but an officer stationed outside had stopped him from going any further. Brent didn't say it, but I know if that officer wasn't there to stop him, he would have killed my dad for what he'd done to his sister.

We didn't do much that Christmas Day after opening presents, and my brothers and I didn't say much. We were exhausted and just wanted to wake up from this bad dream. No one wanted to talk about the night before.

Later that evening, both my uncles were back at Tron and Kelly's, and they were out in Tron's shop, which had a TV and a big work area. Oftentimes, we would hang out there and have our family get-togethers for birthdays and special events. That evening, I started to walk outside to join them. When I got close, I could see through the window. I saw Devin talking to my uncles, and he started sobbing. My uncle Brent hugged him as he continued to cry.

Without my family there with us, I don't know what we would have done.

CHAPTER 12

"I'll cut your throat, mutha fucka!" a man yelled from across the room from where Devin was sitting down playing spades with some of the other patients.

A male nurse quickly ran up and tried to calm the situation by getting between the two men. The three other men and Devin continued playing cards like there was nothing abnormal about the situation, because frankly it wasn't abnormal for the place Devin was at. He was at a state-run rehab facility in the Twin Cities area, and it was a place where prison inmates went as a part of their sentencing. Devin said there were men who came from prison who said they'd rather go back to their jail cell than be at "this hellhole."

Devin was there and not at a more professional facility for a number of reasons.

It had started about a year earlier when Devin was at my mom's house. Mom came home from work one day and found Devin unresponsive in the basement. She thought he was dead and called the ambulance for help. They arrived, and it turned out Devin had overdosed on some benzos. If my mom hadn't found him when she did, he would have definitely died.

After the incident, Mom and Devin agreed that he would go to rehab and hopefully work through some of the stuff that he'd avoided about my dad.

Devin ended up going to the same facility our dad went to, Hazelden. When he got there, he immediately refused any of the possible help there might have been after meeting a sixteen-year-old kid who was there for marijuana use. His rich parents in California had sent him there because of his "marijuana addiction." This pissed Devin off, and he was vocal about it.

"You have a kid in here for marijuana? Are you kidding me? You're going to sit here and put him with people addicted to heroin and pills? A kid just experimenting with a little grass? This is BS, man. He's here because his parents paid you."

The therapists didn't appreciate Devin saying all of this in front of the other patients, but Devin had a point. Talk about insulting on several different levels to have a literal kid thrown into a group of adults addicted to pain pills and crack cocaine, when really, this sixteen-year-old just needed some actual parenting. But that's not ultimately what got Devin kicked out of Hazelden.

After less than a week at the center, Devin received a package from Emma. Inside was $400 worth of pills. Even though Devin had no hand in the package, he was kicked out. They ended his stay at Hazelden immediately, and he was soon back home with my mom. Whether Emma sent the package to purposely get Devin kicked out, or whether she delusionally thought she was helping Devin by supplying him drugs in rehab, it clearly hindered any progress Devin could have had in a place like that.

It wasn't long after that when Devin found himself in the hospital on a seventy-two-hour hold. Generally they do this when someone is suicidal or a threat to themselves and their own well-being. Devin wasn't suicidal, but when he was found passed out again, he was taken to the hospital and kept for evaluation. He said while he was there, it was easier than ever to get the pills he liked. All he had to do was walk up to the nurses' station and claim he was feeling extreme anxiety, and within a minute, he had the benzos he wanted. He didn't even have to go to a drug dealer. He got them in the hospital.

This is often the case in our very sick society, though. The legal drug dealers, doctors and pharmacists, are all able to profit off of and enable drug users, and nobody bats an eye. I saw it with my own eyes working in medicine. I can't tell you how many active-duty members I personally helped take care of who were addicted to pain pills, and as sure as the sun rises, they would come in every few weeks to refill their meds with some new ailment. They would try to get an ADHD and/or depression diagnosis for the benzos, Adderall, Xanax...they immediately got access to almost any drug they wanted. All because of legal drug dealers who are supposed to look out for their patients. Eventually, once the patient was confronted about their overuse of pills (if they were confronted), then the patient would hit up the emergency room a few times, before eventually finding themselves on the street scoring pills.

I want to be very clear that some people truly need these drugs; I've taken care of those people too. But the medical system is so easy to game for these drugs, and I saw it over and over and over again. If you are able to make lifestyle changes to better your situation, please do that before you take a pill. For yourself. These drugs are no joke. And don't forget the dollar sign and incentive on your head when someone wants to prescribe them to you.

Even with the perk of free drugs whenever Devin wanted, he didn't want to be there.

"You know this is bullshit. You guys are holding me here against my will," he told the doctor.

"Careful," the doctor said.

"No, I'm serious. You guys are taking what I say out of context and using it against me. You do that all the time around here. I see it everywhere. I don't want to be here."

"Watch it. I'm serious," the doctor said again.

"No, you guys take a stand-up comedian who makes a joke about suicide and you could claim he's a threat to himself and you could hold him against his will. I'd be surprised if you guys haven't done that before."

"All right, you're staying," the doctor said.

Not long after that, Devin was at a state-run rehab center with a bunch of other people who didn't want to be in rehab. At a place like Hazeldon, most people wanted to be there. There was order among a group of people wanting to get help and truly change. This place was the exact opposite. Only a handful of people wanted to be there. The others were there because the judge said they had to be.

One of the men Devin started to play spades with every day was named Dream, which wasn't a nickname. Dream was from Washington DC, and he was in the pseudo rehab center for crack cocaine as a part of his prison sentencing for his drug charges.

"The hell they put you in here for, Devin? You definitely don't belong here," Dream said one day.

"Yeah, well, I don't really have a choice."

A man named James spoke up from across the table. "Were you dealing drugs? Judge send you here like everyone else?"

"Got kicked out of another place, and this was really my only option. No judge," Devin said.

They laid their first set of cards in the round, and James's partner trumped his winning card.

"Are you stupid or something?! I will beat your ass playing like that." James stood up, chair sliding out from beneath him. "You know who I am?!" he said pointing at his partner sitting across from him.

"Chill man, I messed up. Sorry. We can still win," his partner said. "I can win every hand but one, man. Chill."

"Last son of a bitch who crossed me I tied him up by the ankles in Nevada and put him behind my motorcycle and d—"

"DAMN, JAMES! SHUT UP!" Dream said, grabbing him by the shirt and forcing him back down into his chair. "Are you trying to incriminate yourself or something? Damn, bro, relax. He messed up, let's play. Let's see if he's got the cards."

The men Devin played cards with were real-life criminals and most of them gang members, at least that's what they said. James was a member of the Hell's Angels, and claimed that he was so badass that the Hell's Angels refused to let him be a part of the group until he could prove he wasn't such a loose cannon. Devin didn't know if he was telling the truth or just posturing, as a lot of the people did who were just getting out of prison. The harder you came off, the less likely you were to get messed with in prison. But most of them forgot they weren't in prison anymore. James was also there on drug charges, and after a few days of playing cards with him, Devin started to think that maybe James's brain was stuck in some sort of acid trip. He wasn't as big of a space cadet as his old friend Tree in Colorado, but his stories were over the top, and James seemed to believe every word was true.

Then there was Dream. Devin said he thought Dream was the only other sane person in the whole program, and because of that, he talked to him every day during and after cards. As he got to know him, he found out that Dream was a part of the Black Guerrilla Family. The BGF was a gang that started in a prison in the 1960s. It started as a way to "promote black power," "maintain dignity in prison," and "overthrow the United States government." According to Dream, he had seen murders where men who crossed the gang had their manhood cut off and put in their own mouths before they were shot in the head. He was explaining how hard the gang was after Devin had asked him what it was and how he had got to the rehab center. Devin didn't know if Dream said it to intimidate or just as a matter of fact. They were in a rehab/therapy facility, so Devin thought maybe that was him sharing whatever was in his mind that was bothering him. Apparently, he trusted Deev enough to tell him what had messed him up since childhood.

"So was it like that in prison too?" Devin asked one day when they were sharing war stories.

"Oh yeah, guys were stabbed for looking at each other wrong. But that is where they become your family, and you look out for each other. You need each other or you are done." Devin couldn't believe some of his stories. "What about you? A little white boy from white-ass Minnesota? Have you ever stabbed a motha fucka?" Dream said, laughing.

"You'd be surprised, man," Devin said, going along with Dream's razzing.

"Yeah right. You're lying," Dream said.

"I had to, man. If I didn't, he would have killed her."

"Holy shit, you serious? Damn, Devin. I would have never guessed. Who was she?"

"My mom."

"And your dad?"

"Yep," Devin said.

"Shiiiit. See, you know what prison is like then. Sometimes you gotta do what you gotta do."

Devin didn't know why he had just told Dream that. Usually he kept everything about Dad to himself. It felt good to tell Dream about it. In a weird way, they were similar, and Devin felt like Dream might actually understand him. Hell, if half the stuff he'd said was true then he definitely was able to understand him.

"So let me ask you this. He's in prison for that, right?"

Devin nodded.

"Why in the actual hell are you here with a bunch of real felons? Some of these motha fuckas here did worse stuff than your daddy. You a damn hero for saving your mom, and you here? Like a criminal?"

Devin thought for a bit and finally replied, "I told you. I got kicked out of Hazelden because Emma sent me a bag of pills."

"Man, shut the hell up. You know exactly what I'm saying. You shouldn't be here. What are you, twenty-two? Get the fuck out of here."

"Shouldn't I say the same thing about you? About anyone here?"

Dream shook his head. "In my head, I didn't have a choice. I had nobody, and if I could live a life without seeing some of the things I seen, I would. Sounds like you got people who love you, that's all I'm saying. You want to be like your daddy in prison?"

In the middle of their conversation, the elevator door opened and inside laid a man, seemingly trying to stand up but unable to.

"Help!" said the man.

"Ahhh hell no," Dream said. "Yo, Kendrick down again. Where the nurses at?"

Devin looked over and saw a man in the elevator covered in his own waste and blood.

"Hey, new girl, careful he got AIDS," someone said to the nurse as she ran to the elevator.

It was one of the more grotesque things Devin had seen since he'd arrived, but it wasn't surprising.

During his last few days at the facility, Devin thought about what Dream had said. Maybe he didn't belong at one of these places...or maybe he did. The thing that struck him most was what he'd said last: "Want to be like your daddy?" That pissed Devin off, and it was the last thing he wanted to be compared to.

"What the hell am I doing?" Devin asked himself.

OCTOBER 2014

I had four months left in San Antonio, and I was sitting in my TAP class, which stood for "Transition Assistance Program." People who are leaving the military, whether it's for retirement or expiration of the four-to-six-year contract, must attend this week-long class. It's meant to help you prepare a resume, apply for unemployment, and discuss what other benefits you may or may not be eligible for when you are a civilian. The truth was I was just there because I had to be. It was a nice week away from the clinic on Lackland, and I got to sit and think about the book I was writing at the time.

I hardly took leave at all during my four years, and I had so many leave days saved up that I would be getting out two months before my contract expired in March of 2015. My plan at the time wasn't much of one. Once I got out, I was going to be staying at my mom and Brent's for a few months while I finished my new book. The only hard plan I had, beside finishing my book and selling it to a publisher, was to drive out to Colorado with an old friend from high school to see if I wanted to live there. Devin had lived out there, and the one time I'd finally talked to him he told me it was awesome. I knew Devin had been to rehab in the Twin Cities, but we didn't talk much about that, and I had no idea what his whole experience was while he lived in Colorado. My plan in Colorado was then to check out some of the schools in the area, and that was if my book didn't sell. I had a great feeling about my idea, and I thought it would get bought up right away. It was inspired by one of my favorite books, *Catch-22*, a satire on the military during World War II, and my idea was to write a new satire about the modern military.

Instead of sitting in my TAP class and working on my resume, all I did was daydream. I thought about my story and what else I needed to write to fix the plot holes, then I thought about what I would do after my book was a success. I would then start working on my next book, hopefully have some skits and funny videos produced, all while hiring my brothers and Chase and Dylan, if they still wanted to be a part of what we'd started building years before. I was more motivated than ever to make everything a reality. By joining the military, I'd opened a window of time for myself, and I was going to take full advantage of it.

I wouldn't have been working on my book with two months left in the Air Force if it hadn't been for my friend Daniel. I was going to write the entire thing after I got out of the military, but when I'd told Daniel about it a few months earlier, he'd asked me, "Why are you waiting? If you want to do it, just start now." He was right. Why be one of those New Year's resolution types and wait to start? So I did.

I always liked running my ideas past Daniel. He was creative as well and usually saw my ideas from a different angle, adding to them and forcing me to think about them differently, which generally made the idea better.

I met Daniel when he and his wife moved to Brainerd in 2008, the fall of my senior year. My mom has always been the "more the merrier" type person, and whenever there were new employees at her clinic, she tried to make sure they felt welcome, especially if they had moved from out of town. Daniel and Janelle moved from the Twin Cities, and it would have been one of their first years away from the cities during Thanksgiving. Mom invited them to our house, and they joined our family that year, along with some of our other family and friends.

After dinner, my brothers and I showed Daniel a few of our home videos, and he thought they were hilarious. When he laughed, we showed him more, and soon enough, he was giving us ideas for more videos. A few weeks after Thanksgiving, Daniel asked us to come help out with some painting and odd jobs at the house they had just built. While we were there, Daniel told me about a book idea he had. We brainstormed on it, and I told him about a few of the ideas I had for movies and other funny skits. From that point on, whenever I had an idea, I would call him and run it past him. I once heard that for every good idea, there are

1,000 bad ideas, and in order to find those good ideas, you need to throw everything at the wall with other writers and bring no judgment to the table. Telling someone, "That's dumb" or "What an idiotic idea" creates a cancerous collaboration. If the idea is worth exploring, the conversation continues. If it's not, the conversation moves onto the next topic. This is how we operated.

The other thing Daniel and I talked about a lot was the military. Daniel was a paratrooper in the Army, and when I decided to join the Air Force, he came with my mom and me to the recruiter's office. I wanted someone there who knew about the tricks recruiters try to pull. For example, trying to get someone to sign up for six years versus four years. Each branch needs to recruit so many people or the military fails to operate properly, which I understand and support, but having a quota each month on the number of kids you are supposed to recruit just did not sit well with me. I saw way too many people in the military who shouldn't have set foot in the recruiter's door, but they were enlisted because the recruiter needed to meet his numbers.

When I got out of the military, I called Daniel and asked him about his transition from military to civilian life. Although our experiences were different, the institutionalization of the mind is the same, and sometimes the transition can be tough, even without any combat experience. If you do have combat experience, the transition can be excruciating.

In January 2015, I took my trip to Colorado and decided it wasn't the right decision to move there. I spent the next few months at my mom's, and I finished my 75,000-word novel. It was one of the hardest things I had done, and I was proud as hell of what I had written and completed. I'd written stories before, and I'd created a ton of things, but this was different. I felt like it was a mental marathon getting up and writing 1,000 words a day minimum and then cleansing my mind in the evening to do it again the next day. When I finished, I submitted my manuscript to ten agents and publishers every single day for two months. I created a Twitter account and did everything I could to tweet at other authors and agents to get their attention and hopefully garner interest in my book. It was now May, and I received only two responses. One agent requested a chapter and another requested three chapters. They both passed on it.

I was absolutely deflated. For months this was my only plan. All in on it. My mind was engulfed in this project. It was all I cared about, and in the end it was shit. Nobody wanted it.

Once reality set in about my creative endeavors, that maybe I wasn't supposed to be creating anything at all and that maybe I was just a delusional dreamer, the world around me started to come back into focus. I was officially two months out of the military, and I had no job, no plan, and no book to sell anymore. I began to actually miss the military. Beau had joined the Navy the year before, and for a little bit, I thought maybe rejoining and getting stationed near him would be cool.

I called Daniel one day and told him, "Dude, I gotta rejoin, I think. I don't know what else to do. I'm going to do pararescue."

"Get the hell out of here. You don't want to do that and you know it," he said.

Daniel knew what stage of the cycle I was in: Someone joins the military, and in the first six months to a year, that person is gung-ho about his service. He sees all the possibilities of his career. He's just completed training and is excited to get out there and excel in his new job in the military. Pride in his new identity is worn on his sleeves wherever he goes. Then, year three comes around, and that same person has seen the bureaucracy and absurdity around him. He sees the politics involved in promotions. He doesn't like it, and he can't wait until his contract is up. His contract expires, and he gets out into the civilian world, finally, and he realizes he no longer has the giant support system he'd had just a few months earlier. He doesn't have the structure, the camaraderie, or the purpose, and the VA is a giant mess... For the next year he plans on rejoining, until he finally does rejoin or finds another purpose away from his once very important purpose serving in the military.

This was me to a tee. I was lost when I left the Air Force, purposeless, and desperately trying to figure out what my next step would be. I called Daniel a lot to talk to him about it, because I knew he could relate.

Instead of rejoining, I decided to move into a house in the cities with two of my best high school friends while I attended the University of Minnesota for accounting. After my failed book, I had pretty much thrown in the towel on the dream room and any possibility of film school. I realized that I had to become a cog in the corporate wheel or be a lazy turd that could never provide for my future family, and I wanted a family more than anything one day. I could spend months writing another one of my book ideas, only to have it not sell like the last one and be right in the same position, or choose the cubicle. I chose the cubicle route out of fear of never being successful in the creative world. It's shameful looking back on it.

When I started attending classes again and living in the cities, I was forced back into the social spotlight, and when that happened, I started experiencing something I hadn't experienced yet. Every place I went, I expected to turn the corner and run into my father. Every place. When I went to Target, the grocery store, the gas station—I was constantly in a state of paranoia. What would I say to him? What would he say to me?

Eventually I started to withdraw again. I had researched my professors before signing up for spring classes to see which ones had mandatory attendance and which ones didn't, and I took any fully online class that I could. This way, I wouldn't have to go to campus anymore.

I started dating frequently using dating apps with the sole purpose of finding a serious relationship. There is a stigma about the apps where people, mainly old timers who dated before the internet, think the apps are only used for hooking up, but that is not the case. At least it wasn't in my experience. I knew I wasn't going to hang out at the bars and find a woman there, and at the time, I was not going to church, so the apps were simply a ticket to dinner or coffee, and if there was chemistry, there'd be another date. If not, then no date. It was that simple. I wanted to get married and have kids, so I knew I had to go on dates, as much as I hated to go out and be social.

Every girl I went on a date with, I did the same thing to avoid the conversation about my real dad. I just told them my dad was a machinist and left it there. Problem solved, I thought. I didn't like it, because it felt dishonest, so on one date, I tried explaining what happened with my dad in 2007. I didn't know how she would react or what I should even tell her. As I started, I could sense my heart rate rising and my breaths getting deep. It felt like Christmas Eve morning when I was in Japan. When I realized I had little beads of sweat on my forehead, I stopped the conversation and tried to change the subject altogether. I just told her that maybe we'd talk more about it later and that I didn't want to scare her off. It felt humiliating reacting like that in front of her, in public no less. She wanted to go on another date, but that was the last one we went on.

I felt myself regressing back to my shell, and instead of going to class with the intention of getting my degree, I just took classes to get my GI Bill money to live on while I trained to rejoin the Air Force as a pararescueman. We know a lot about Navy SEALs because of Hollywood, and because what they do is very intense and very honorable, but pararescuemen are even more badass, in my opinion. They are combat paramedics. When Navy SEALs go down behind enemy lines, PJs go in and save them. They have a two-year training pipeline called superman school, and the washout rate is 90 percent. The washout rate for Navy SEAL training is about 80 percent. Whenever I saw PJs running on Lackland Air Force base—while I was training people about to get kicked out of the military for being out of shape—I thought that's where I belonged, with them. Running ten miles a day and preparing themselves to go save people. "That others may live" is their motto. It's what I needed to do, be one of them. I needed to do this for myself, and I needed to have that purpose in my life, I told myself. I needed something to be proud of, and that was it. I knew I was very capable of it physically too. I got 100 percent on my PT tests, which was very rare in the Air Force, and mentally I excelled in all of my other training, so I knew I was a perfect fit.

In my room, I got a whiteboard and kept track of my personal best times for swimming, running, pushups, and sit-ups, and I started training. I swam or ran every day and increased my strength in the evenings lifting weights at the gym with my roommates. I emailed a recruiter and talked to him about finding others training in my area who I could connect with. I was dead set on rejoining and planned on doing it within the year.

During that final year before I rejoined the Air Force, I attended school online and spent time fishing and golfing with my roommates. The only other social life I had was working with Daniel. I got the job when the event company he was working for needed help one weekend during an event in downtown Minneapolis. The event was for a large corporation's charity drive. Our job was to set everything up, be there to shift props and tables around during the gala, then break it all down afterward and get it out of the building. It was simple work, not overly complicated, and it was exactly what I needed at the time. It was the first time since I left the Air Force that I felt like I was part of a team again, and I enjoyed it a lot. We had a mission, and we all busted our tails to accomplish it that night. I had worked many jobs before the military, but this one was different. It wasn't like we clocked in at 3 p.m. and went home at 11 p.m. I enjoyed this job.

After that, I was asked if I could help on almost every event they had in the next few months, which was awesome for me, because there were local things we worked at and events in Alabama, Miami, and New York City. On these longer trips, our job was to transport everything to the event site, set it up and work the event, then break it down and drive it back to Minnesota. I was getting paid to see the countryside while I did my school work. It was perfect.

Driving with Daniel felt a lot like fishing and sitting on the jungle hill with Denson in Japan. We went for hours sometimes without saying a word, and other times, we discussed politics and sports, and other times, we laughed until I felt like I broke a rib. I didn't know it then, but Daniel's friendship was exactly what

I needed at the time too, and on one of our first trips, I came to learn that we had a lot more in common than I'd ever realized.

We were driving to an event in Florida, so our road trip was almost a three-day drive. When we were driving through Memphis, I started noticing that Daniel wasn't quite acting right. He was quiet, seeming almost paranoid, and when I tried to talk to him, he was often unresponsive. It's like his mind wasn't even in the same place. He was in la-la land.

"Dude, what the hell is going on with you? I've never seen you like this," I said.

"You gotta drive. I can't drive," Daniel said.

This was very abnormal. We'd driven to all four corners of the country in Daniel's truck hauling stuff, and this was the first time he'd ever asked me to drive.

I drove from Memphis to the Florida Panhandle, where we got a hotel room that evening, and once we checked in, Daniel didn't say a word. He went and laid in his bed with his shoes on, just staring into the abyss.

I had no idea what to do. "Should I take you to the hospital, man? Are you okay?"

"I'll be fine," he said.

I texted his wife to see what I should do. She told me he had anxiety sometimes, and if it got too bad to bring him to an emergency room.

The next morning, Daniel was a little more with it and able to drive us to Miami, but when we finally got there, his mind was even worse than the night before. He was mute. Catatonic almost. Just sitting there in his own mind. Finally, another group member and I convinced him to go to the emergency room, and after we dropped him off, I didn't see him for the rest of the day.

The next day, aside from breakfast, I didn't see him either. He skipped the event completely and stayed in his room and slept.

On the third day, our group moved to another place to stay for a few days. We would work one of the days, then stay at a small resort in one of the Keys as a group "vacation" day. Daniel finally came with us on that last day, and he seemed like he was pulling out of whatever he was going through. I was relieved and finally able to ask him about what was going on.

"You all right, man? What the hell is going on? You don't have to tell me, but that was pretty scary, dude. I was worried something was seriously wrong. I even texted Janelle a bunch asking what I should do," I said.

"Yeah, I'll be all right. It just happens every once in a while. Not like that usually, but it happens."

"What exactly was happening? I literally thought you stroked out or something. Back when we were in Memphis, I asked Janelle if I should bring you to the hospital."

"No, not a stroke, thankfully. They diagnosed me a while back with PTSD from some stuff in the Army."

"Damn. Does this happen to you often?" I asked.

"No, not crazy often. But when it happens, I just can't get out of it. Like when we were driving? My mind was just racing. I could hear you talking, but it just wasn't computing. I was just thinking about everything. It's weird that it happened over twenty years ago, but it still sticks with me like it was yesterday."

I didn't say it, but I knew exactly what he was talking about. This was almost exactly how I felt when my mind snowballed. There was no escaping the snowball once it started. Usually I had to fall asleep and hope I woke up without it rolling still. What he described was how I felt.

I didn't ask Daniel about what had happened that caused him to go into those zombie modes. I figured if he wanted to say anything about it he would, and vice versa. He didn't know my family when everything happened with my dad, but I know he knew of it in summary, and he never tried to prod things from me about it, and I appreciated that.

We spent the rest of the weekend at the resort with all of our coworkers, and Daniel slowly came out of his fog and was able to enjoy the time there. When we were done, we drove the truck and trailer home, and once back in Minneapolis, we unloaded the truck and went to get some lunch before I went home.

We were driving to an old taco place in the heart of Minneapolis, and on our way there, I felt the anxiety building up. Like usual, once I'd moved to the cities, I had this underlying paranoia that my dad would be at the restaurant. I would catastrophize in my head about the possible situation and how I would respond. How would I escape if I had to? But this time, for the first time ever, I felt like I could tell someone about it.

"You know what's really weird, man, and I almost feel silly saying this, but every time I'm out at the store or a restaurant or something, I get this knot in my stomach and this feeling that as soon as I walk in, I'm going to be staring at my dad. It doesn't even make sense. I don't even think he lives around here," I said. It felt good to say it out loud.

"What's he going to do if you see him?" Daniel asked.

"I don't know, honestly. That's the thing I think about."

We drove a little further in silence, both of us thinking about what I'd said, and for some reason, I just started telling more.

"This one time, I had to get my braces when I was fourteen. My dad drove me there in the morning, higher than a kite. When we would stop at the stoplights, he fell asleep. I'd wake him up, and every time he'd wake up, he'd get pissed. When we got there, he passed out again in the waiting room in front of this girl I used to like. Talk about humiliating, man. Not sure why I thought of that, but yeah, whenever I'm out in public and I think about running into him, I think about that type of stuff for some reason and it just starts to snowball. It's weird. Like you said earlier, the memories just start running, and the snowball is impossible to outrun."

"Have you ever told your brothers about that?" Daniel asked.

"Just when it happened. We got home, and I told Devin about it, and he said, 'Oh my gosh, that happened to me the other day too.'"

"Ever tell your mom?"

"No. The only person I told was Devin. That was about ten years ago now."

"No lie, I think all of that is some PTSD stuff there, man," Daniel said.

We drove a little further until we got to the parking lot of the restaurant.

"So I see a therapist for this stuff, right?" Daniel said. "She's pretty cool. Sometimes we just sit and chat about whatever. It seems to help quite a bit, honestly. I'm not sitting here telling you that's what you need, just FYI, but she told me this old story about an Indian tribe, way back before we knew what PTSD was and shell-shocked soldiers. These Indian warriors would go off to battle and do and see God knows what, and when they would come back they weren't right. They would wake up at night seeing ghosts, and their wives couldn't figure out what was going on. The weirder thing was when these warriors went back out with their fellow warriors to hunt or train, they were fine. Almost like nothing happened. No ghosts, nothing.

"You know that saying, blood is thicker than water?" Daniel asked.

I nodded.

"A lot of people think that means blood of family, but it doesn't. The saying refers to blood on the battlefield being thicker than water in the womb."

We sat in the parking lot for another minute.

Daniel finally broke the silence. "Let's go get some tacos."

I hopped out of the truck and walked into the restaurant, forgetting all about the possibility of running into my dad.

CHAPTER 13

When I look back on the people who have come in and out of our lives, the timing of their acquaintances is hard for me to brush off as coincidence.

In the spring of 2016, I was preparing to contact the recruiter, I was still dating here and there, and I was ready to be done with school forever. I hated it. I was in classes with a bunch of eighteen-year-old kids, and it was virtually impossible to connect with any of them. Frankly, I didn't want to. School, as I already knew, was not for me. I could have grinded through it with good grades and gotten my piece of paper with the school seal on it, but I didn't want to.

One thing that I did regain while I was in school was my creative outlet. When I had given up the dream, I thought I was done forever. It was a waste of time, I'd convinced myself. But while riding with Daniel to a few more events that spring, we started making our own satirical articles, like *The Onion*. Instead, we called our publication "The Garlic."

It was all for fun, and that's all I expected out of it, but it resparked the long-shot dream in the back of my head that maybe, one day, I could make entertaining articles and stories a career. At that time, though, it wasn't the driving force behind making our articles. I realized that I needed to exercise this part of my brain, because when I did, I felt good about it. Knowing that I made something that would elicit a response (hopefully laughter) made me feel like I was doing something worthwhile. It was a part of me, and I needed the outlet no matter what I did going forward.

With "The Garlic," Daniel and I created a small following online and the content was pretty hilarious, sometimes offensive, but people who were offended made the jokes even funnier. Comedy is supposed to make fun of everything, to find humor in the darkest of places, and to make us laugh at things we're not supposed to—at least that's what I'd surmised from studying my favorite comics. Laughing when you aren't supposed to makes the jokes even funnier. We made no money off of our site, but we laughed until we cried a few times writing the articles. I felt like I was making something worth making again, even if our content was only making us and a handful of lunatics online laugh, and I loved it. It would be easy to continue while I trained for pararescue, I thought.

One thing I was disappointed about with my potentially leaving again was just missing Devin, who was relocating to the cities with his fiancé and would have been living really close to me.

After Devin completed his stint in the state-run rehab facility, he moved to Thief River Falls to be around the rest of our family and go to school. He completely cut ties with Emma and told himself he was never going back to one of those places again.

He chose to make changes in his life, and as soon as he did, his life changed forever, for the better. While he was in Thief River Falls, he met a girl named Uma, who he quickly fell in love with. They would end up moving out to Dickinson, North Dakota together, where they got engaged. Soon, they would be moving to the cities, which meant we'd get to hang out again finally (if I didn't end up rejoining the Air Force). We hadn't lived in the same place since I had left for college eight years earlier. Devin and Uma were also getting married that summer.

Devin would be the first of us three boys to get married. The next summer, Beau would marry Haley, a girl he fell in love with while he was serving in Boston on the USS *Constitution.* I would end up being the last, but it wouldn't be much longer after.

One day, I got a message on my dating app that said, "wow, I'm so glad you survived that paper cut, it must have been terrifying, how long were you in a coma from that?" It was from a girl named Tessa. She was responding to my profile description where I detailed that I was a "paper cut survivor." Stupid I know. I had a good reason for putting that joke in there, to attract a girl with a similar sense of humor.

As corny as it was, Tessa thought it was funny. She likes to say that I bailed on her "TWO TIMES" when we had dinner scheduled, but the third time was the charm. We met at a sushi restaurant in Uptown, a neighborhood close to Minneapolis. I thought she was gorgeous, and when we started talking, I really liked her personality too. She laughed about my stupid joke in my profile, and I told her about "The Garlic," and she thought that was funny too. Since she liked that, I told her about everything else I liked to create.

I learned her family had a little hobby farm growing up, which reminded me of my grandparents' farm, she was into sports like I was and was even a collegiate diver (and a good one, going to nationals), and she had a similar sense of humor. I could tell halfway through our date that I wanted to see her again. I knew for sure I was going to ask her out again when the topic of our parents came up. Instead of ignoring the subject or lying to her and telling her what my stepdad did for work, I told her the truth. I told her my dad was not a part of my life, and I told her why. I didn't go into crazy detail, because it was the first date, but I told her...and I was fine. No beads of sweat or embarrassing moments. I was comfortable enough around this girl to tell her the truth.

Before we even left the table, I tried to get the next date scheduled, and just a few days later, she came over to my house, where I made her stir fry and we had a fire. I had already fallen head over heels for Tessa. I was so confident in wanting to be with her that I invited her to Devin's wedding even though we had been dating for only a few weeks by that time. She fit right in with my family at the wedding, and that's when I knew I wanted to be with her forever.

When I first met Tessa, I told her about my idea of pararescue, and we even went to work out together at the pool while I did my swimming drills. After a while I started to think that maybe my idea was a terrible one. If I wanted Tessa to be my wife, going through a two-year training pipeline and getting deployed every six months wasn't very conducive to a marriage. I had seen firsthand how hard that was for marriages. The divorce rate was insane. I also knew that if I wanted her to marry me, I had to figure out my career situation and fast.

In an online comment thread, I heard about air traffic control and how their training process worked, that it didn't require a degree, and you could make almost $200K a year once you were done with training. All you had to do was get through the training, which is easier said than done, but I applied, and a few months later, I got accepted into the training program for "Center." Most people think of the "tower" when they hear "air traffic control." A center is who your pilot is talking to when you are 30,000 feet in the air and coming in to land.

I didn't know a lot about being a controller, but they said I'd learn it all at training...in Oklahoma City. There were now a couple of problems with this job. One, the training was about six months and in another state. Two, when I finished, I had no control of where I would end up working, kind of like the military. Three, I wasn't guaranteed a job. I would have to complete the training, and the washout rate was almost 50 percent. I wasn't as worried about number three. I knew if I studied and put the time in, I could do it. I wasn't stupid. But I was worried about number one and two. I had been dating Tessa for about six months, and I wanted to be with her, but I was afraid to ask if she wanted to come with me and potentially scare her away.

I finally thought, *Screw it, I have to ask her what she thinks. If she says no, then I will find a job somewhere else.* I knew I could get a job being a job recruiter or something, if I really had to.

We were driving on highway 169 to our favorite sushi restaurant, and I said to her, "So I got accepted into the air traffic control program, but the training is in Oklahoma City for about six months."

"Oh my gosh, congrats!" Tessa said. "Six months isn't too long. Will you be able to come home on the weekends if you want?"

"Well, I was hoping I wouldn't have to do that. I want you to come with me."

She sat and thought about it for a few seconds.

"Okay," she said.

She worked it out with her job to work remotely, and a few months later, Tessa and I moved to Oklahoma City where I would train to be an air traffic controller.

Although I was no longer paranoid about running into my dad and I wasn't having public panic attacks when I flashed back to old memories, I still hadn't dealt with my memories, and I wasn't quite sure how to. Talking about it with Daniel and Tessa seemed to help a lot, but not fully. I still felt a cloud in my heart. I told Tessa a summary about my dad being in prison and why he'd ended up there, but I still didn't fully open up. One night at my house, before we moved to Oklahoma, she asked me about it, and I tried to tell her about that night, but I struggled. I only gave her snapshots and answered her questions with minimal detail.

I was still so angry with my dad when I thought about everything.

Why? Why would you do this to us? I'm now with an amazing woman named Tessa, and I'm supposed to have you there for advice. How do I ask her to marry me when I'm ready? Should I ask her dad? Should I let her pick out the ring or just get what I think she will like? Is this job I'm applying for a good idea? Instead I'm trying to figure out how to talk about this BS and hopefully not scare her away. Screw you, Dad, for not being here for me right now.

From that night in 2007 until the time I was dating Tessa, I wasn't just mad at Dad for what he'd done, I was angry with God. For a while, I even decided that maybe God wasn't even real. How could God let his children suffer? The amount of suffering in this world is immense, and if he was all powerful, why would he let any suffering exist at all? From Jamal, to Sergeant Smith, to Dana, to my grandpa. Why did he put people through such pain? The only time I went to church in that ten-year span was when I had to go with Mom and Grandma, and in basic training so I could get out of the barracks and away from the Hulk, Sergeant White, for a few hours a week. Other than that, I completely cut God out of my life.

Even though I cut God out of my life, his messages still found a way to get through to me exactly when I needed them, whether I recognized them as divine or not.

One evening, Tessa and I were watching a movie called *The Shack*. We had just moved to Oklahoma City, and I was starting my training for air traffic control. Janelle, Daniel's wife, had recommended the movie to us. As we watched, I found myself connected to the main character. His tragedy was horrific, but like him, I was questioning my faith after something bad hit my family. He was angry with God just like I was, and as the movie goes on, his relationship with his father is revealed. He hated his father when he was drunk, so much so that he poisoned him when he was a kid to make it all stop.

He is forced to empathize with his father and see what he'd gone through as a kid. This made me think about my own father and his relationship with his family.

My dad grew up with an alcoholic father and gambling mother. He used to tell us stories about the times he and his brother got in trouble. They were close in age just like Devin and me. One time, when they were five and six, they piled up some socks and underwear and lit it on fire. Obviously, this is a terrible thing to do and should be punished. That said, their punishment was getting burned with a lighter to teach them a lesson. My dad would also tell us about how he played baseball and hockey growing up, but his parents only ever came to one game, and his dad was shit faced and screaming, "Hit the mother fucker" from the stands until he was finally removed from the arena. On Thanksgiving one year, his dad got so mad and drunk that he grabbed the turkey right off the table and threw it out into the yard in the middle of dinner. When Dad was twenty, his brother got into a car accident that left him with permanent brain damage, and just like that, the brother he knew was gone forever. A few years later, his mother died.

As I watched the movie, I thought about Dad's childhood and the hardships that he'd dealt with, and I started to cry. None of this justified my dad's actions, but for the first time, I began to empathize with my father's own pain. I thought maybe this was why he'd done some of the stuff that he did while we were growing up. I tried so hard to hold it in next to Tessa, but I couldn't.

Then the movie talked about forgiveness.

I had heard so many people talk about forgiveness, and I understood what it meant, but I didn't know what it felt like to truly forgive. I saw this character going through his process of forgiveness, and I felt like it was showing me what I had to do in my own life. Holding onto this hate for my dad had absolutely destroyed me, and it had prevented me from both growing personally and in my relationships.

I needed to figure out how to forgive my dad.

"Just say it out loud," said the character.

I had removed God from my life, but his message of forgiveness had still found me when I needed it most. When I'd needed a mentor and a friend to guide me through my times in Japan, I got one in Densen. When I'd moved home, given up on my creative hobbies, and fallen into another hole, ready to leave for the military again, I'd desperately needed a friend, and I got one in Daniel, who helped me deal with my flashbacks and memories. When I'd decided I was going to keep the stuff about my dad buried away while dating and I needed a woman I felt comfortable enough around to open up to, I got one in my future wife, Tessa. When I was truly ready to forgive and needed to hear the message of forgiveness, I got it in a movie.

I never said it out loud, but over the next few months, I said, "I forgive you, Dad" in my head every day, and slowly I felt a weight lifting. This horrible event in our past was long done with. It didn't change the fact that he'd altered the course of our lives forever, but I truly forgave him. I wished no ill will on him for what he did. I choose to remember the good times I had with my dad and the good things he taught me. It didn't mean I wanted to rekindle a relationship with him, but I forgave him, and I loved him for giving me the good things that he did. He was, and still is, my dad.

The other person I had to forgive was myself. I didn't quite know how to do this. I said it out loud, but I needed to talk to Devin. He and I had hardly talked at all about that night, but we needed to.

One day when I was visiting home from Oklahoma, we went fishing, and we started talking about his days in rehab and in Colorado. He told me all about Emma, Tree, and Dream, and I told him about all the times I'd had flashbacks, how, for years, I'd felt terrible about not going back inside with him that night. As the older brother I should have been the one to do what he did and not him.

"It's all right, man. We both did what we were supposed to that night. And we're all okay," Devin said.

"I just feel guilty, man. Had I gone in there instead of you, then maybe you wouldn't have had to go through all of that," I said.

"I've never held anything against you, ever. You got us out of there that night. We were a team, and we both played our part. Don't feel bad about anything."

And that's all I needed to hear. That night on Christmas Eve, we'd played the roles that we had been raised to play. I was always planning for every scenario, and my planning that night got the three of us boys out of the house safely to get help. Devin was fearless in everything and lacked regard for consequence, and on that night, he was fearless and did exactly what he was supposed to do.

CHAPTER 14

I STARTED THE ZEDUCATION YOUTUBE CHANNEL ON OCTOBER 2ND, 2018, but we have to flash back a little bit to the true start.

When Tessa and I were in Oklahoma City in 2017, I continued to collaborate with Daniel on our satirical articles. We wrote very few toward the end of my training because of how intense the classes were. The information in the program wasn't overly complicated, but it was a lot to learn in a short amount of time, and not only did you have to fill in bubble sheets, you also had to apply the information to real-world scenarios. The pressure was on to pass, or you were back out onto the street without a job. One thing I was shocked to learn was that there were college degrees available for becoming ATC, but those people who got degrees still had to take and pass the course just like someone off the street like myself with no degree. So, for those people who spent $60–$100K on a four-year degree, the stakes were even higher.

More than 80 percent of your grade came from three "problems" on your final two days of the course, and you had to finish with 75.1 percent overall or higher. The "problems" were mock scenarios where you spoke on radios with fake pilots and other controllers to guide fake planes through fake airspace safely. One single mistake could cost you 5 percent of your grade, so if you made a handful of mistakes, you were left without a job, even if you'd spent four years and accumulated $100K in debt getting a degree. It still seems criminal to me that anyone was allowed to get a controller degree when the federal government would treat them like cattle regardless of their obvious commitment to the career. It is still one of the most inefficient, wasteful, and bizarre training setups I have ever encountered.

During the buildup to the last two days of testing, I studied my ass off. Every single day. Tessa was able to work from our apartment, and had I not had her with me every day after class, I would have gone insane.

When I found free time, I tried to keep creating funny articles with Daniel, but our motivation on the site dwindled, until one day, Dylan messaged me.

"Hey man, I love your website. You should see what I have been doing on Twitter. I think I'm onto something."

At this point, Dylan and I hadn't talked in a while. Once I joined the military, I lost touch with almost everyone I knew from before, so I was surprised to see Dylan even knew about our website.

I went to Dylan's Twitter account, and he had amassed more than 100,000 followers tweeting about current events. I couldn't believe it.

"Dude, what have you been doing?! That is incredible, man!" I said after I called him right away.

"Twitter is amazing, and people like what I've been saying, apparently. You and Deev are literally the only ones who thought this was cool. All of my other friends think I'm wasting my time."

"Wasting your time? Dyl, you're talking to one hundred thousand people. That's insane!"

After that, we chatted almost daily about the possibilities of collaborating in the future. Dylan loved our articles, and I loved making humorous content about current events, sports, and pop culture.

As excited as I was about it all, I had to put it to the side and focus. I needed to pass these problems and get a job as a controller. If I passed, I would be assigned to a control center. My class would find out what places were available after we all finished the problems on the last two days. At that point, I didn't care what locations there would be, I just wanted to pass first and then worry about where Tessa and I would be going. There is a center in Minneapolis, so we kept our fingers crossed that it would be on our list. The more people who passed in our class, the better. That meant more assignments would be available. Heading into the last week, we were down to sixteen people from eighteen. The previous two classes had had five people out of eighteen pass and four out of eighteen. The prospects of a big list were not great.

Finally, the day came to run our first problems. I would run two of my three problems on the first day, so it was crucial to kill them and get the pressure off for the last problem on the second day. The simulators look exactly like you would expect: a dark room with radar equipment lined up on both sides of the wall with twelve stations total. When I walked in, I approached the remote pilot and my co-controller, the two who would be simulating the problem for me. The grader sat behind me just over my shoulder. My heart raced. I hated the anxiety, but I remembered what my dad had taught me during wrestling: be confident in the work I have put in, and when the bell rings and the match starts, the butterflies will go away. Besides, this was a nothing burger compared to some of the stress I had been under before. I can do this, I told myself. I knew I could.

The problem started, and as soon as I made my first radio transmission, the butterflies were gone. "United 212, Flight Level 2-3-0 approved…" I went for a half hour, directing aircrafts around the airspace, giving them radio frequencies guiding them safely along while I was in control. There were other students around me all speaking, but I was in the zone, focused solely on my monitor and the tasks in front of me. The problem ended, and I felt incredibly confident in how I did.

"I got a sixty-four for you," said the grader.

Damn, I thought. I thought I'd killed it, and with that score combined with the written tests during the first sixteen weeks of my grade, I was sitting at about 69 percent overall. I needed to crush my last two problems.

I did the second problem that day.

"Eighty," said the grader.

Not bad, I thought. An eighty on any of the problems should have been good, but the score of sixty-four on the first one put me in a tight spot for the next day. It meant that I needed an eighty-two or better to pass the course with 75.1 percent.

I showed up the next day expecting to ace my last problem. That was my mindset. I'd worked my butt off for sixteen weeks, and I was going to move on. I got into the simulator and began the problem. About three minutes in, I made a transmission, "Delta 310, Flight Level 2-3-0 approved," and I immediately knew

I'd messed up. The flight level should have been 2-5-0. The direction I gave made the aircraft clip a restricted airspace, which they counted as a plane crash. A colossal mistake. The max I could score after that mistake was an eighty-five, and I still had thirty minutes left of the problem.

Screw it, I said. *I'm going to ace the rest of it.*

I got into the zone and did exactly as I was trained to do, not worrying about making another mistake that would ultimately wash me out of the program if I did.

"Eighty-five, well done," said the grader. "You passed!"

I started floating on a cloud. I couldn't believe how much weight I had been walking around with until the moment I heard him say that I'd passed. It was one of the hardest things I had done up to that point, and passing it remains one of the most gratifying things I've ever felt. It was the ultimate learn and apply course, and I had just passed it. Our class was an anomaly during that time in Oklahoma—eleven of the eighteen of us ended up passing.

I called Tessa immediately to tell her the good news, and when I did, she started sobbing. She was so happy. Not only was the work hard for me, the entire process took a lot of work and sacrifice for her too, and to see it pay off that day was just as gratifying for her. We had dinner as a class that night, and it was the best tasting steak and old fashioned I've ever experienced.

The list of centers was minimal, and I was forced to work at the center in Oakland, California. Tessa and I agreed that we would do it for a few years and hopefully be able to transfer to the Minneapolis center. This was our plan anyways...

When I got to Oakland, I was shocked to see how I would be spending my time. I thought I would get there and immediately start training to become a certified controller, but that was not the case. All new trainees spent three weeks memorizing their new airspace maps and call signs, then they would sit around for up to a year waiting to simply start training, which would last about two to three more years. All in all, it was about a two-and-a-half to three-year process.

"So when can we transfer?" Tess asked.

The answer was never, or "maybe in about twenty years." But we didn't know that right away.

After I sat in the classroom for three weeks and passed my map tests, I went down to the floor. Every day, I would show up and plug into the control area in my section to listen for a bit if the controllers on duty would let me, then I would try and study. The rest of the time, the other students waiting to train sat and talked. One of the unspoken rules was acting like you wanted to be at the center, which 95 percent of the students there didn't. Nobody wanted to live in the Bay Area, where the cost of living was to the moon and homeless people were living on every corner. Controllers who worked there made more than $200K a year but were still driving two hours *each way* every day to work just so they could own a house. It was insane. It was an absolute backlogged mess at the center, which left it well under the national average for staffing levels. After a few months, I would learn that nobody was allowed to transfer out of Oakland unless staffing levels were above the national average... Oakland would never be over the average, because nobody wanted to be there.

As I sat around for months getting paid to wait to start training, I started working with Dylan on his newfound Twitter popularity. I started my own Twitter account and wrote funny skits for our new YouTube channel. I loved talking about politics and current events but wanted to do the best I could to be humorous about it. There were enough people regurgitating talking points, so I wanted to try and keep it light but also get my opinions across.

When I created my Twitter account, I decided to not use my real name for a number of reasons. One, I was a federal employee, and I didn't want it to affect any chances I had with my upcoming training. I was in a liberal mecca, and if someone found out I simply owned a gun they might not train me without bias. Two, my real name is hard for people to say—not Desmond, but Janousek. I think I have heard it said about 1,000 different ways. Three, as a movie junkie, I always thought it would be cool to create my own pseudonym. Jamie Foxx, for example, was born as Eric Marlon Bishop. Jamie Foxx sounds much more interesting. Brad Pitt was born as William Bradley Pitt. The list of famous people who do this is endless...and if I ever got a chance, I wanted to make my own. I even did so when I submitted my book manuscript. I wrote as "Desmond Tyler." I decided that was boring too, and I wanted to shorten my alias even more, so I used my middle name, Tyler, and I flipped my nickname around, Dez, and got "Zed." Tyler Zed would be my alias. As I continued waiting to start training or to get transferred to another center, I would write skits and funny tweets and think of things Dylan and I could do with our growing platforms on Twitter.

A few months into sitting around at the center, I would find out about the national staffing levels and that certified controllers had been waiting to transfer for over ten years. I couldn't believe it. Plus, the controller world is all about seniority, so I definitely wasn't transferring, ever... I'd have to become the top dog with time logged and then hope the staffing levels went up. Thinking about it realistically, I realized it wouldn't ever happen. Tessa and I would have to stay in California forever.

Then one of my friends told me about a way a few trainees had been getting around the system. He told me he had a package to transfer already. This was shocking news to me, because everyone around me pretended to want to be there, even him. Secretly, everyone was scheming to leave.

"Allergies, man. Go to this doctor and get the allergy test to all things native to California. Say your allergies prevent you from functioning well at work and they'll transfer you. I'm leaving in like two months," my friend said. He went on to tell me about several other people who had done it before him.

It's genius, I thought. Everyone is allergic to something, and if the plants are native only to California, the solution is to transfer you where those allergens don't exist. These bureaucrats can't say no. Whatever the guidelines say, they do. Like robots...although very slow most times.

I got home and told Tessa about the new plan, and she was thrilled. There was no way I didn't have at least a few allergies. Back in Minnesota every spring my eyes swelled up and I sneezed like crazy. I was even allergic to bees. I was going to have at least a few allergens on the test.

No doubt, I thought.

I scheduled the test, and a few days later I was in the clinic getting poked in the back by about thirty little pins with different allergens. I sat for a bit, then the doctor came in to tell me everything I'm allergic to.

"You're good to go. No allergies to native California allergens," he said.

"No. Way," I said to myself.

As I drove home, I dreaded having to tell Tessa the news. When I got home and told her, she slumped down on the couch.

The idea of living there forever was setting in, and we were both absolutely dejected.

That evening, we sat and talked about what we really wanted. We wanted a house, we wanted kids, we wanted our family to be involved in our kids' lives, and realistically, that wouldn't happen in California. It was not a place we wanted our kids to grow up in, either. We lived in a nicer area of a town called Fremont, and right behind us lived three homeless men on the city bike path. Everyone knew they were there, and it was just a part of everyday normal life. Needles littered their encampments, and we were just supposed to be okay with it. It was not a place to raise a family.

We either stayed in California and sacrificed what we wanted for my job, or I quit, and we moved home, where I would figure out something else.

We decided that sacrificing our families was not worth any job in the world, no matter how much it paid, and the next day, I walked into the training office and told them I was giving up my training spot, and that was it. A month later, Tessa and I drove home, and Daniel and I drove back out with his trailer to get our stuff. As scary as it was to not have a job to be able to support us, luckily Tessa had a great job already. I told myself I'd get a job at McDonald's if I had to. I'd rather do that than live where we were living for the next twenty years and not be able to be with the people we loved.

Once home in Minnesota, it didn't take me long to get a job. Daniel's brother-in-law had just bought a printing business and took me on as a project manager. I had no idea what the hell I was doing in the print world, and it wasn't a prestigious job, but it paid well, and I was incredibly grateful for the opportunity.

We were home in Minnesota, I had a job, Tessa was able to work from the office again, and I was able to work with Dylan more on our budding platforms. We had a few dozen skits and even started a podcast that lasted ten episodes. Our content wasn't quite there yet quality wise, but we were building something, and getting the creativity flowing again felt amazing. We even brought Devin and Chase into the mix with our shows. It felt like when we were kids chasing the dream room again.

As our platforms grew and grew and grew, so did the visions we each had for the future. Dylan had a giant voice in the conservative movement and was getting phone numbers of people on Fox News all the time and receiving invitations to speaking events. It was insane to see. As we toed the line with these bigwigs in political media, the more I felt I was straying from the vision I'd had in my mind, the one that I'd felt good about. I didn't want to be a serious talking head in the winless political fight of left and right, and that's where I felt it was headed. I wanted to talk about these issues but do so with humor. I wanted people to come to my pages and hear about some of the problems in the world, but not leave with a blood pressure of 200 over 100.

In late 2018, we decided to do our own things as far as our platforms. Dylan kept on his path, and I started my channel on YouTube called Zeducation.

After I saw the potential, I became obsessive over YouTube. I knew that each platform had an algorithm, and according to all of the information available, if you studied your analytics and kept improving every video then the algorithm would start recommending your videos. I also truly enjoyed making my videos. I loved sharing the things I found interesting and important and funny, and I wanted to attract people who had the same interests as me. One of the best things I heard when I had less than 1,000 subscribers was, "Don't stop making videos. Just don't. No matter what."

And I didn't.

I committed myself to doing three videos a week, minimum, and starting in January of 2019, that's what I did. I did three videos a week about all sorts of topics, from politics to Hollywood hypocrites to people acting irrational. Highlighting the absurdities in our culture and doing my best to make it humorous with my edits and reactions to these things. Each video I posted got ten to twenty more views than the previous. Then it was 100 to 200 more. Then 1,000 to 2,000. The next thing I knew, I had tens of thousands of people subscribed to my channel and watching my videos. I knew it was possible when I started, but I couldn't believe it was actually happening like I had envisioned. The most important thing to me was that people were watching and actually enjoying my videos. It was an amazing feeling that I had only dreamed of just a few months before.

Eventually, my channel started making money. Enough to where it could replace my salary at the print shop, with the potential of earning more. When I showed Tessa the earnings, she said, "Maybe you should do this full time."

There was no hesitation from her, there was no worry, she was all on board and supportive of me. Without her backing of me, Zeducation would have ended a long time ago.

So I quit my full time job and committed myself to my channel. It was a leap of faith, but I was confident it would work. "Just keep making videos," I always reminded myself.

Soon enough, I got to the point where I needed help with everything, and I hired Devin in early 2021. He quit his full-time job and came to work for me full time. Also a leap of faith on his part, but he believed in it and was just as committed as I was.

Over the next few years, we grew the channel, busting our ass every day creating videos. Literally sun up to sun down we were working on content. Eventually we hired an editor, Meagan, and Chase and Daniel even had a stint as full-time employees for the Zed Media company. Eventually we hired Beau. In December of 2022, four years after the channel was created, Zeducation hit 1 million subscribers and continues to grow every single day.

As I write this, I sit in the studio we built. My set behind me, our equipment in front of me. In a few minutes, Deev will be here, and we will go live in front of our audience like we do every morning, and after that, we will work on videos for the week for Zeducation and the new Deev channel that is closing in on 100,000 subscribers. Everything we escaped to growing up—to our forts, to our videos, to our business ideas—is now something we live out in real life every day.

The dream room.

CHAPTER 15

I sped to the hospital. My heart raced. I didn't want to break any laws, but I wanted to get there as fast as I could.

"Please, God, let everything be okay. Please be with us," I prayed. I stayed as calm as I could. Getting overly anxious or excited was not going to help anything. I had to be solid in that moment, level headed. Calm and collected.

We got to the hospital, and we waited and waited and waited.

As we waited, Tessa's blood pressure dropped, and her monitors started beeping warning sounds and lights.

"Tessa. Hey, can you hear me?" said the nurse who ran into the hospital room. Tessa's consciousness began to fade. Her blood pressure plummeted, and my level of worry reached ten out of ten.

"Keep talking to me, Tessa," said the nurse. The nurse began hurrying in what she was doing. She took the epidural catheter out of Tessa's back and injected her IV with something, I didn't know what, but Tessa started to come back.

I breathed a sigh of relief.

About an hour later, the doctor came in and began speaking with Tessa about what was going to happen next, and a few moments later, two assistants came in and helped the doctor.

"Okay, now push, Tessa!"

In less than twenty minutes, on February 4th, 2022, Quinn Diane Janousek came into the world.

My breath stopped when I saw my daughter for the first time. For nine months you prepare yourself for that moment, and for me, I felt like I had been preparing for longer. All I wanted was to be a dad, but there's no preparation for that feeling when you see your child for the first time. In that moment, I felt immense pride in the new responsibility I now had as a father. To teach, provide for, and protect this little person. I needed to be the best dad possible. I needed to be the strongest pillar in this girl's life, just like my family was for me.

The doctor held Quinn as I cut the cord, and as I looked into Quinn's little eyes, I did everything I could to hold back my joy, but I couldn't. I began to cry seeing her. I had never felt happier.

I sat and watched my wife hold my daughter, and I finally fully understood my purpose. My family, my anchor.

ACKNOWLEDGMENTS

I WOULD LIKE TO THANK A FEW PEOPLE FOR MAKING THIS BOOK possible.

First, thank you to my agent, Lindsay Guzzardo, for her guidance and hard work on the manuscript. From pitching the book to publishers, to editing, and to helping me fine tune the details of the story, this book would not have been without her expertise.

Second, Debra Englander and publisher Post Hill Press. Thank you for believing enough in this story to publish it.

Third, the Zed Team. Thank you to Devin, Beau, Meagan, and Daniel for getting things done with content and merch while I wrote this book. Without you guys I don't know what I would have done.

Lastly, to my wife. Without your unwavering support and love, I wouldn't have had the strength and courage to finally write this.

ABOUT THE AUTHOR

TYLER ZED (REAL NAME DESMOND JANOUSEK) WAS BORN IN Minnesota in 1990. He served in the United States Air Force as

a medical technician from 2011 to 2015. After getting out of the military, he attended the University of Minnesota where he began creating YouTube videos as a hobby under the alias "Tyler Zed." Years later, his channel, Zeducation, has garnered over a million subscribers and continues to get millions of views a week.

Amanda Nippoldt Photography